Description

A BUSY WRITER'S GUIDE

Marcy Kennedy

Tongue Untied Communications
ONTARIO, CANADA

Marcy Kennedy
marcykennedy@gmail.com
www.marcykennedy.com

Book Layout ©2013 BookDesignTemplates.com
Edited by Chris J. Saylor
Cover Design by Melinda VanLone

Description/ Marcy Kennedy —1st ed.
ISBN 978-1-988069-10-4

Contents

Why a Busy Writer's Guide? 1

How Much Description Is Too Much? 5

The Description Myth...5

Genre Considerations...6

Defining Description..7

How Point of View Brings Description to Life 9

Demystifying Point of View................................10

How Does This Matter for Writing Description?......12

What We Describe...12

When We Describe It..13

How We Describe It..13

Making Description Serve the Overall Story.............17

Ground the Reader in the Setting 18

Symbolize or Foreshadow 20

Enhance the Theme..21

Add Subtext 22

Build Characterization 23

Amplify Emotions 23

Add Conflict, Tension, or Complications 24

Hint at Backstory 26

Placing Our Description in the Right Spot 27

Recognizing Purple Prose and Other Problematic Description 29

Ten-Dollar Words 30

Clichés or Clumsy Figures of Speech 30

Flowery Abstractions 31

An Abundance of Adjectives and Adverbs 32

Are Adjectives and Adverbs Always Evil? 33

Characteristics of a Good Description 37

A Good Description Is Specific 37

A Good Description Uses the Five Senses 38

A Good Description Allows Less to Be More 39

A Good Description Shows Rather than Tells 40

The Five Senses In Fiction 43

Helping Readers See Your World 49

Avoiding the Tom Bombadil Problem 50

Allow Your Character to Put a Twist on It 50

Put What Your Character Sees Into Motion...............51

Break Expectations by Playing with Opposites 53

Exploit the Scope of What Our Eyes Can Take In 55

Use Gender Differences 55

Focus on "The One" Rather than on "The Many".......56

Give Order to the Description 58

Using Sound to Make Your Novel Stand Out in a Sea of Noise 61

Use Words that Sound Like Their Meaning...............62

Play with the Emotional Effects of Sound...................63

Let Sound Set the Mood 65

Include Background Noise...65

Extra Tip...66

Using Taste to Make Readers Hungry for More 67

Decide When Naming a Taste Is Enough 67

Use Metaphors or Other Comparisons........................ 68

Make It Surprising Somehow... 69

Use the Full Scope of What We Can Taste 69

Don't Limit Yourself to Describing Taste Only When
Your Character Is Eating or Drinking 70

Consider the Outside Factors that Influence Our
Perception of Taste 71

How to Make Your Novel Scratch and Sniff.............. 73

Describe a Smell When It's Fresh 73

Use Smell to Alert Your Character to a Change or to
Impending Danger 74

Connect the Smell to an Emotion................................ 74

Choose One "Showpiece" Scent 75

Contrast a Good Smell with a Bad One 76

Using Touch to Pull Your Reader Into Your Novel... 77

Use All Aspects of Touch 77

Explore the Non-Physical Touch 79

Observe (or Break) the Continuum of Intimacy.........79

Consider How Your Character Will Interpret It........83

Metaphors and Similes..85

How to Create Memorable Figures of Speech.............85

Mistakes We Can Make with Figures of Speech 88

Describing Setting..93

A Quick Reminder 93

Fill Your Setting with Extras..94

Share What Makes Your Setting Unique......................95

Include What the Reader Might Get Wrong..............96

Make Your Setting a Reflection of the Person Who Lives There 98

The #1 Secret 98

Bonus Tip...99

Describing Characters...101

Describing a Non-Viewpoint Character 101

Describing a Viewpoint Character............................106

Extra Tip...108

Describing Actions and Reactions 109

    External Action 109

    Internal Reactions 114

Take It to the Page 117

Showing and Telling 127

    What Do We Mean by Showing? 127

    What Is Telling? 130

    Why Is Showing Normally Better than Telling? 130

Other Books by Marcy Kennedy 133

    For Writers 133

    Fiction 138

About the Author 139

Why a Busy Writer's Guide?

A FEW YEARS AGO, I STARTED CREATING *Busy Writer's Guides* for a very simple reason—I wanted to give hope and practical help to writers who were struggling to reach their goals and dreams because of the demands life placed on them.

This became my passion because I know what it feels like to be overwhelmed by responsibilities that can't be ignored or delegated and to prioritize the needs of those I love over my own desires. I know what it feels like to make it through a day with no energy or creativity left to write.

And I knew I couldn't be the only one. The more writers I talked to, the more I found so many others who felt stretched too thin. They were trying to fit writing in around full-time jobs or around caring for children or aging parents or grandparents. They were battling physical and mental health problems. They had life commitments that were as important to them as writing.

They were people who wanted to achieve their dreams, but who didn't want to do it at the cost of their health, their relationships, or their moral compasses.

While I can't solve all the problems in the world, or in anyone's life, I wanted to help make writing a great book more achievable for those people—people like me.

And that's where the *Busy Writer's Guides* were born.

They're short, yet in-depth and practical. The intent is to give you the full coverage of a topic that you need to write well, but to do it in a way that still respects your time.

How does that work?

These guides leave out the filler and fancy prose padding meant to impress you. My goal isn't to make you think I'm fantastic. My goal is to help you become fantastic. I cut the fluff while keeping the substance so that you can have more time to write and more time to live your life.

Each book in the *Busy Writer's Guides* series gives you enough theory so that you can understand why things work and why they don't, but also enough examples to see how that theory looks in practice. Approaching it from two sides like this streamlines the learning process and speeds up your learning curve.

In addition, these guides provide tips and exercises to help you take what you've learned to the pages of your own story with an editor's-eye view. There's a leap we all need to make from intellectually understanding a topic to proficiently applying that topic to our work. The Take It to the Page sections give you a way to start, trying again to make this transition easier and quicker for you. If you're not ready to apply it to your work yet, you can skip these sections and come back to them later.

The final way that I try to respect your time is by separating some topics out into appendices. A lot of writing craft concepts overlap. I try my best to keep the material in the body of each of my books fresh. In other words, I minimize the content overlap between books as much as I can without sacrificing clarity. (In some cases, I still do have to re-explain elements or I wouldn't be doing justice to the concept at hand.)

When I think there are elements of other topics that aren't absolutely essential to understanding the current topic, but which would help you understand the topic of the current book better, I add them as appendices. That way, if you've read my other books and don't need a refresher, you can save time by skipping the appendices. If this is the first one of my books you've read, or if you want to refresh your memory on a topic, you can read the appendices.

And that's quite a long enough intro, I think. Time to get to the meat. If you want to find out more about me, you can visit my website at www.marcykennedy.com or check out the About the Author section at the end of this book.

CHAPTER ONE

How Much Description Is Too Much?

O NE OF THE MOST COMMON QUESTIONS when it comes to description is "how much description is too much?"

This is a valid question. Without enough description, we leave the reader feeling ungrounded. Actions take place in a white bubble of nothingness. Too much description can slow our books down so that the reader grows bored and moves on to something else.

The problem is "how much description is too much?" is a nuanced question and isn't the best question to ask if we want to write an excellent book.

THE DESCRIPTION MYTH

Description is the red-headed step-child of the writing craft. It's undervalued and almost feared because writers tend to believe that things like dialogue and action are inherently better. We start to believe this because we associate dialogue and action with being active and interesting and we associate description with being static and boring.

Those are false dichotomies.

As a freelance fiction editor, I've more often seen people whose books lacked depth and emotion because they were dialogue heavy than I've seen people whose books were too slow due to excess description.

Dialogue doesn't necessarily make our stories better. Good dialogue does. Bad dialogue makes our writing slow and boring.

Now here's the fact we need to understand—the exact same thing is true about description. (And about every other element of the fiction writing craft.)

Good description is vibrant, interesting, and active. Bad description is slow and boring.

So part of answering the question of "how much description is too much?" comes down to setting aside the myth that description is somehow less interesting or less important to our story than other elements.

GENRE CONSIDERATIONS

The genre we're writing in influences how much description we'll need.

For example, cozy mystery, historical fiction, science fiction, and fantasy readers all expect and want a higher level of rich sensory description in their stories. Comparatively speaking, thriller readers want less description (or, at least, description of a different kind, but more on that in a minute).

If we don't give readers what they want, our books will fail.

This means that another part of answering "how much description is too much?" depends on knowing our genre. What do readers of our genre want?

DEFINING DESCRIPTION

Description isn't de-valued only because of the false dichotomy created between description and other elements of fiction writing. It's also de-valued because many times it's assumed—incorrectly—that description is merely recounting the physical appearance of the setting and the characters in it.

Description does cover those physical appearance elements. It also includes the other senses (sound, smell, touch, and taste) and action (both internal and external).

Yes, you read that right. Action is actually a subset of description. It's description in motion.

Most of this book focuses on helping you master the more "traditional" sensory description because that's where the majority of us struggle, but I'll also be lightly covering action description. Until we reach that section, when I say "description," I'm talking about sensory description unless otherwise stated.

So rather than asking "how much description is too much?"—which implies that it's a necessary evil or a virus we need to minimize the spread of—the questions we really need to ask are "how should we use description in our story?" and "how can we make description as interesting as possible?"

Answering those dual questions is what we'll spend the rest of this book doing.

CHAPTER TWO

How Point of View Brings Description to Life

POINT OF VIEW IS THE PERSPECTIVE FROM which a story is told. If we're writing our story from a limited point of view, then we can't talk about description without talking about how it interacts with point of view. Why? Well, in a limited point of view, there's no such thing as objective description. All description filters through the viewpoint character and is colored by who they are as a person.

That idea underlies almost everything else I'm going to teach you in this book. Because of that, let's quickly run through a point of view (POV) refresher.

DEMYSTIFYING POINT OF VIEW

Point of view can easily confuse writers because the term refers to two different elements of writing.

It refers to the overall perspective structure that we'll be using for our story and, if we chose to go with a limited point-of-view structure, it refers to how we maintain consistency to that point of view and what character we chose as our viewpoint character.

Let me break this down so that it's actually clear. (If this is material you're already comfortable with, feel free to skip down to the *How Does This Matter for Writing Description* heading. But sometimes a refresher can help even those of us who are well-versed in POV.)

One of the first choices we need to make about each story we write is the overall perspective structure—a.k.a. point of view—that we'll use to write the story. Assuming we're writing genre or mainstream fiction rather than experimental fiction, we have four options.

Omniscient point of view is when the story is told by an all-knowing narrator who is not a character in the story. The omniscient narrator can tell the reader what any of the characters is thinking or feeling, and they can even describe things that the characters don't know about. Omniscient POV is different from having multiple viewpoint characters. In omniscient POV, you only have one point of view (or viewpoint) and it's that of the omniscient narrator. The reader hears only one "voice" in the narrative—that of the omniscient narrator.

Second-person point of view uses *you* in the story rather than *he* or *she*. In other words, it places the reader in the position of narrator. The story is ostensibly happening to the reader themselves, and only what the *you* character experiences can be included in the story. Second-person point of view is normally only used for choose-your-own-adventure-style fiction.

First-person point of view uses pronouns like *I, me, we, us, mine,* and *ours.* Just like it sounds, in first person, the character tells the story directly to the reader. Unlike with omniscient POV (where the narrator is also speaking directly to the reader), the first-person narrator is a character within the story. The first-person narrator can only share information and experiences that they are aware of. They can't share things outside of their perspective. The story is told in the "voice" of the viewpoint character-narrator.

Third-person point of view tells a scene, chapter, or sometimes even the whole book from the perspective of a single character, but it uses *he/she* instead of *I.* The balance between the author's "voice" and the viewpoint character's "voice" depends on how close or deep we choose to go into the viewpoint character. In deep POV, the author disappears and the reader hears the viewpoint character's voice just as they would in a first-person story, except for the pronoun difference.

Once we decide on the overall structural point of view, we have to select the viewpoint character or characters. This step doesn't apply to second-person POV, but it does apply to all the others.

The narrator for omniscient point of view could simply be the author or it could be a created character external to the story like Death in *The Book Thief.* Remember, omniscient POV stories will have only one narrator and viewpoint.

In first-person and third-person POV, we can have multiple viewpoint characters if we want as long as we transition properly between viewpoint characters to avoid what's known as head-hopping.

So the scene by scene point-of-view choice we have to make is about whose consciousness we're going to experience the story through.

(If you want to learn more about point of view, I recommend you read *Point of View in Fiction* and *Deep Point of View*.)

HOW DOES THIS MATTER FOR WRITING DESCRIPTION?

Second person, first person, and third person are all considered *limited* points of view because the reader will receive the story through a single character at a single point in time, the same way we experience our own lives. Everything that goes on the page must be something that the viewpoint character would have known, thought, or experienced. That limits what we can describe.

It also influences how and when we describe *everything*.

WHAT WE DESCRIBE

Working through the perspective of a viewpoint character means that we'll only be able to describe items they notice.

The tricky part of this for us is often when we want to describe something the viewpoint character is familiar with. We don't tend to think about things we see or use every day. This includes the structure of our social system or what our best friend looks like.

What they notice will also be largely influenced by their circumstances. A character heading into a job interview will be hyper aware of their own appearance, whereas a character who's crawling around in a cave looking for hidden treasure won't. A character who is running for their life will notice different things about their surroundings than will a character who isn't in immediate danger.

If it's not something they would notice, then we either have to leave it out or come up with a believable, realistic reason for them to notice it.

This also provides a helpful framework for us if we're not sure what to describe. We can ask ourselves questions like…

What in the environment is new to my viewpoint character?

What might my viewpoint character not notice because they're so familiar with it?

What do they care about?

What's important to their overall story goal or their scene goal?

How does their personality/background influence what they notice or ignore?

WHEN WE DESCRIBE IT

Fiction is governed by cause and effect and action-reaction sequences. An easy way to think about these from a practical standpoint is triggers. Something happens and that triggers something else to happen. I spill water in your lap, and you jump out of your seat and scowl at me.

What this means for description is that we should describe things when our viewpoint character notices them, not before and not long after.

For example, our viewpoint character (let's call her Sarah) goes to her high school reunion. Her ex-boyfriend hugs her. If he smells like sandalwood, she'll notice that almost immediately. She won't notice it ten minutes after the hug has ended and they're talking about their jobs.

HOW WE DESCRIBE IT

The *how* is where description becomes both tricky and fun. It's all about the voice.

Voice is a fancy writer term for how personality and individual perspective influence the way in which something is said (or, in our case, written).

We're exposed to different voices every day. If your mother, your ten-year-old son, and your best friend were part of the same event and told you the story later, each of them would describe it in a different way. The basic facts would be the same—maybe a band played a concert in an outdoor stadium—but what they noticed, their word choices, their sentence structure, and their emotional interpretations would vary.

So when we're writing description, we have to take into consideration the voice of the viewpoint character.

How does our viewpoint character's background influence their description? A former Marine might describe the rain on the window as sounding like machine gun fire. A chef might describe the same rain as sounding like steak sizzling on a pan.

How do our viewpoint character's emotions about the situation, person, or item color their description? Take, for example, a character revisiting their childhood home for the first time in five years. If they had a happy childhood, that will color the way they describe the setting. If they had a miserable childhood, that should come through as well.

Remember that *why* a character is noticing something will influence not only what they see but also how they feel about it. A butter pecan cupcake with vanilla icing will be seen differently when it's celebrating a new job compared to when a woman's husband refuses to stick to his weight loss program despite his growing health issues. People also tend to spend more time noticing (describing) things they feel strongly about, positively or negatively.

How does our viewpoint character's knowledge affect their description? We don't all know the same things. Two characters might ride the same city bus and one identifies the foreign language being spoken behind them as French. The second only knows it's a foreign language that sounds pretty. Or think about the difference between the way a mechanic and a pampered teenage girl would describe a problem with a car's engine. Education and life experience play a role in the words our character uses.

When it comes to how our viewpoint character's voice colors description, the basic guideline to keep in mind is that our viewpoint character shouldn't simply be cataloguing the world around them the way a camera would. They should be interpreting it through the unique lens of who they are.

CHAPTER THREE

Making Description Serve the Overall Story

WE COULD HAVE ALSO CALLED THIS section *The Purpose of Description* or *Does Your Description Deserve to Exist?* Everything in fiction needs a reason to exist. Descriptions that don't serve a purpose in the story except to allow the writer to enjoy their descriptive skills are purple prose, something we'll look at in more depth in the following chapter.

Irrelevant description is what gives description a bad name.

You might think that's obvious, but so often in my editing work, I've seen authors describe things in detail that have no bearing on the story at all. Usually they do it because they've been told at one time that they weren't including enough description and no one told them what *kind* of description they needed to start including or how to properly include it.

I'll give you an example.

Say our main character is a children's aid worker who enters the home of prospective adoptive parents for the first time. In every house, there are hundreds of details we could include. The color of the paint on the walls. The placement of the furniture. The style of the furniture. Whether there are paintings on the walls. And on and on and on.

But what would actually matter to that scene? Details that say something about the people living in that house as it relates to whether or not they'd make good parents.

Description is about more than moving the characters through the scenery. It's one part of a larger whole, and so we need to think about it in terms of what it can do on top of providing a sensory experience for the reader.

In order to justify its existence, every passage of description should do two or more of the following things:

- ground the reader in the setting (time, place, and/or culture) so that they know when and where they are
- symbolize or foreshadow something important to the story
- enhance the theme
- add subtext
- show something about the viewpoint character's personality
- show the viewpoint character's emotions
- add conflict or complications
- hint at backstory

Let's look at each of these in more detail.

GROUND THE READER IN THE SETTING

Every time a new scene opens (whether we're starting a new chapter or staying in the same one), we need to anchor the reader. That means anchoring them within the viewpoint character if we're writing in a non-omniscient point of view. It also means anchoring them within the setting so that they can picture the surroundings.

Where are they? Location can make a difference in how our readers imagine the scene. If they imagine our characters are sitting safely in their camp, and two pages later we reveal that they're actually traveling a dangerous mountain trail, it jerks the reader right out of the story. They have to stop and reorient themselves to how they were picturing the scene (if they were able to picture it at all). They might even be confused enough that they feel like they need to go back and re-read the chapter to understand it. Some won't. We don't want that. Anytime we pull the reader out of the story, it's a bad thing. We risk losing them as readers.

When are they? Day or night? Has a significant amount of time passed since the previous scene?

Who are they with? It's a terrible feeling as a reader to suddenly have a character speak a few pages into a scene and to not be certain whether they were there all along and the writer forgot to mention them or if they just arrived…and the writer forgot to mention it.

Is there anything important around them? We don't need to give the reader every detail of the location, but they do need to know about items that will be pertinent to the coming scene.

These aren't just "boring details." These are the elements that the reader needs in order to be able to imagine the story world and understand what's happening. If we leave the reader basically floating in a bubble so that they don't know what to visualize, they'll be less invested in the story.

The tricky part of grounding the reader in the setting is that it can be less interesting than other material if we allow it to drag on too long and don't combine it with one of the other reasons for description to exist. Description for the purpose of grounding should be quick and needs to happen within the first few paragraphs of a new scene.

If time is the only thing that's changed, we'll need to use even less description than if our characters also changed location.

As a general guideline, describe a place in the most depth the first time that setting shows up on the page. Later on, unless something important has changed, a brief re-orienting passage is enough. The reader will have less patience for a lot of description the second time through.

SYMBOLIZE OR FORESHADOW

Foreshadowing is hinting at what's to come in your story. You can foreshadow a major plot element, the character's internal state or future transformation, or a secret (either not yet revealed or revealed to the reader but not to the viewpoint character) all through little details.

In the movie *Million Dollar Baby*, the writer could have chosen many details to show us future boxer Maggie Fitzgerald's poverty. The detail chosen was a steak. Maggie works as a waitress and, early in the movie, her boss catches her packaging up a steak left behind by a customer. She tells her boss that she's taking it home for her dog, but then we're shown Maggie eating the steak herself.

That detail ties in again later in the movie. Maggie spots a little girl and a dog waiting in a truck at a gas station. That gas station could have been shown using any number of details. But it wasn't a random detail about a man washing his windshield or the smell of gas in the air that the writer chose. It was a little girl and her dog. Seeing that little girl and her dog prompts Maggie to tell her trainer the story of her much-loved father (now deceased) and their German Shepherd Axel. Axel was in so much pain at the end of his life that her father put him out of his misery—and he did it because of how much he loved the dog.

Both of those seemingly unimportant details—Maggie eating a steak she claimed was for her dog and Maggie seeing a little girl and her dog at a gas station—foreshadow what's coming in the movie.

Due to a dirty blow during a fight, Maggie ends up a paraplegic. Things get so bad the doctors have to amputate her leg. She reminds her trainer about what her father did for Axel and asks him to do the same for her. She wants him to put her out of her misery (like a dog), and he does it because he loves her like a father.

Foreshadowing plays a large part in the re-readability of a book.

Symbolism is when you use an object to represent something else or to hint at deeper layers of meaning. In Janet Fitch's *White Oleander*, Fitch uses the oleander plants to symbolize Astrid's mother, who is likewise tough, beautiful, and deadly.

Remember the key when it comes to foreshadowing or symbolism in your description is subtlety. You need to be so subtle, in fact, that not every reader will catch it. But the ones who do will love you for it.

ENHANCE THE THEME

Description, and specifically how the viewpoint character interprets the setting, can be a subtle way to reinforce the theme of our story.

Let's say that over the course of our story our viewpoint character will learn to appreciate her simple, safe life, but at the start of the book, she's feeling trapped, like she hasn't done anything exciting or valuable.

Here's how she might describe her world at the beginning. Ellen is our viewpoint character.

Blake and Angie sprinted outside to their unnaturally square backyard. Ellen leaned against the backdoor, watching them play even though it wasn't necessary. Even if they wanted to, they couldn't escape the confines of the solid wood privacy fence that blocked their yard off from the rest of the world. What kind of person built a fence like this on a block where nothing more exciting than the weekly Neighborhood Watch meeting dared to happen?

By the time she returns to her home after whatever adventures we send her on, she might look at a similar scene and instead describe their backyard as cozy and the fence as wrapping around them (a word choice that suggests a hug).

ADD SUBTEXT

Subtext is what's happening below the surface. It's about imagery and subtlety. It's what's implied but never said.

When we're using description to add subtext, we're going to hint but never state. Not every reader will pick up on subtext in our books, and others will only catch it on the second read-through.

To create subtext, we'll need to be aware of the connotations associated with specific words or items. For example, if we frequently associate a character with the color white, we're implying purity.

Subtext can also be brought out by showing the difference between what our character claims and what they pay attention to. For example, what's the subtext when a woman claims she doesn't want children, but pays attention (shown through detailed description) to adorable little details of the babies around her?

Repeating or echoing certain images plays a part in subtext as well.

BUILD CHARACTERIZATION

What a character notices and how they describe it says as much about the character noticing as it does about the character or place being noticed. We need to remember this double duty whenever we write a description because we'll be characterizing both the person looking and the person being looked at (or the person who lives or works in the location described).

Here's how two different characters might describe the same room.

> **Character A:** The room had a homey, lived-in feel— Beatrix Potter figurines lined the shelves, well-worn books rested next to the arm chair, and the kitchen table temporarily doubled as a place to fold laundry. I'd done the same thing myself more than once.

> **Character B:** The room bordered on needing a Hoarders' intervention—tacky knickknacks on every shelf, stacks of books next to the chair instead of neatly shelved, and the living room table strewn with half-folded laundry. I prayed it was at least clean.

Because description can build characterization on two levels, we have to keep in mind the impression we're building of both characters. Is the impression we've created of both characters what we intended?

We can also intentionally create misunderstandings and false impressions of what's being observed that we'll break later.

AMPLIFY EMOTIONS

If something is important enough for our viewpoint character to notice, one of a couple things is probably happening. Either they feel something about what they're describing or what they're already feeling colors the way they experience the world around them.

I'll give you an example of a description of the same physical thing written first without emotional coloring and then with it.

The dark storm clouds moved in, low to the ground.

How does the viewpoint character feel? It's not clear based on the description.

The bruise-colored clouds swept down so close to the ground that it looked like they'd crush anything in their path.

There's a sense of foreboding in that description. Depending on the context, this is a character who's either afraid of storms or who is feeling frightened or overwhelmed by the other circumstances in the story.

ADD CONFLICT, TENSION, OR COMPLICATIONS

Description can add conflict, tension, or complications in many different ways. We can use it to show something disturbing or threatening about another character. Or our character's surroundings themselves can create obstacles or conflict, like smoke filling the room or a locked door that they need to pass through.

Let's compare two descriptions of the same room. In the first version, we see a flat description of the room with no conflict or tension.

Jennifer ducked into the only other room in the apartment—a bedroom. It had a Captain's bed, an end table butted up to the bedside, and big windows along one wall. Ugly orange and green curtains covered the windows from the top to three inches off the floor. To one side was a tiny, doorless bathroom.

Now, instead, look at the same description when we add the complication that our viewpoint character needs a place to hide and there isn't one.

> Jennifer careened into the only other room in the apartment—a bedroom. The unmade bed was one of those Captain styles with drawers underneath that she'd always associated with kids, not adults. No place to hide there.
>
> Out in the main room, the rattle of a chain marked him locking the door behind him.
>
> She spun in a circle. The only door other than the one she came in led to a tiny bathroom. Without a door. What kind of a person didn't at least hang up a curtain? She glanced inside. Or a shower curtain for crying out loud.
>
> A clatter on the kitchen countertop. Probably keys and a cell phone being emptied from a pocket. If he was like most people, his next stop would be the bathroom. And he'd catch her. And she'd be dead.
>
> She skittered back to the orange-and-green pin-striped curtains that looked like rejects from the sec-ond-hand store her Aunt Bertie owned in the 80s. She ducked behind. Her feet stuck out the bottom. If he didn't look down…please God let him not look down.

The description you include doesn't have to be long to heighten the conflict or tension though. You can do it quickly if that's what the scene requires.

Let's say we have a woman who is visiting her new boyfriend's apartment for the first time. Here's an example of a quick description that increases the tension.

I stepped inside. His apartment smelled like Chinese take-out, Old Spice cologne, and the meaty reek of blood.

By the end of that description the reader will either be mentally screaming at her to run or they'll be wondering why his apartment smells like blood. Maybe a bit of both.

HINT AT BACKSTORY

Backstory is anything that occurred prior to the opening of our story. It can be something that happened to one of our characters or it can be larger world events.

The only time we should share backstory is when it matters to the present-day story. If it doesn't influence the current story in a significant way, then the reader doesn't need to know it.

Backstory also needs to be woven into the story in a way that feels natural. It needs to seem like something the characters would realistically think about or say rather than like something the author shoved in to enlighten the reader. Using description is a useful technique for hinting at backstory or sliding in bits that the reader needs to know.

For example, if a grown woman meets with her father at his office and this is how she describes it, what does it hint at about their past history?

The room reminded her a bit of her father—all neat and dusted on the outside, any mess and dirty secrets hidden away out of sight.

Let's look at one more example. In this one, a man and his dog are moving into an apartment.

I unlock the paper thin door to my new apartment. I could cross the whole place in five long strides. A spider-like crack extends across the far corner of the ceiling, and the bare walls are painted in a shade of dingy yellow that reminds me of a smoker's fingers. Saying it was a downgrade from the four-bedroom colonial Brenda and I bought shortly after we were married would be like calling a tumor a pimple.

Duke pulls back on his leash and whines as if to say *we're not going in there are we?* But we are going in and we're staying because Brenda gave me a choice between keeping the house or keeping the business I'd spent the last five years building while she didn't do anything but sign her name to the partnership papers.

The setting in the above paragraphs serves as the vehicle to weave in backstory about the viewpoint character's divorce and his relationship with his ex-wife.

PLACING OUR DESCRIPTION IN THE RIGHT SPOT

Once we're sure our description does one of these things, we also need to make sure we've placed it correctly. Remember what we talked about in Chapter Two—description should happen only when the viewpoint character would naturally notice those things.

(If you're writing in an omniscient point of view, your job is much harder because you have to decide where to include description without the guiding force of a viewpoint character.)

So, for example, if our character is running through the woods to escape a gunman, he's not going to notice the nest of baby birds or the squirrels hopping from tree to tree. He's only going to notice things that could either help him hide or help him take down his pursuer.

Much of the time, the feeling that prose is overwritten or boring comes from the writer describing things in detail that don't need to be described, that don't need to be described at this particular point in time, or which should have been described differently based on the situation.

This is an important distinction to make. In the example I gave above about a character running from a gunman, you might be tempted to remove all sensory description to keep the story moving, but good description doesn't slow down the story. Good description is necessary to heighten tension and make the story deeper and richer.

Now that we've looked at giving description a reason to exist, and touched briefly on placing it in the correct spot, it'd be easy to assume that whatever we write will be fine. Unfortunately, that's not the case. Description can have a reason to exist and be properly placed and still be poor.

Our next job is to learn how to tell the difference between good description and bad description, and then employ it within our individual writing voice, taking into account the needs of our story.

When we write good description, our readers will enjoy it as much as they do our dialogue.

CHAPTER FOUR

Recognizing Purple Prose and Other Problematic Description

I N THE SECOND HALF OF THIS BOOK, I'LL BE covering tips for specific types of description, such as setting, characters, and action. Before we can get to that, though, we need to understand what qualifies something as a good description and a bad description.

Even if our description serves two or more of the purposes outlined in the previous chapter, it doesn't mean it's good. It just means it deserves to exist. From there, we need to make it strong and beautiful.

The biggest "bad description" offender is purple prose. Don't confuse purple prose with beautiful description (or with description period). Purple prose is writing that's too ornate, overwritten, flowery, or melodramatic. It's self-aware writing.

But it's one thing to define it, and another thing to understand it and be able to spot it in our work. In this chapter, we're going to look at purple prose red flags and other ways that description goes wrong.

TEN-DOLLAR WORDS

A ten-dollar word is one that most people won't understand and that is used as an attempt to make the writer sound more intelligent, more cultured, more "literary," etc. In reality, sentences littered with ten-dollar words usually make our writing stiff and pretentious. If the reader is reaching for a dictionary, they're not sucked into the fictional dream of our world.

The following example is breaking under the strain of the ten-dollar words. You won't always find them clumped together like this. Any of the three offenders in this sentence would qualify the writing as purple prose.

> The mellifluence of her tones triggered deglutition in his esophagus.

Before we use a big, fancy word, we need to ask ourselves why we're using it. Are we using it because it fits the character? Are we using it because it's the best word for the job?

Or are we using it because we're trying to impress someone or sound literary? Are we using it because we think fancy words are what it takes to write well?

If you find yourself using ten dollar words, see if there's a simpler word that will convey your meaning just as well.

CLICHÉS OR CLUMSY FIGURES OF SPEECH

Figures of speech are a big enough topic that I'll go into more depth on them in Chapter Twelve. For now what you need to remember is that a few figures of speech go a long way. Don't pile on multiple metaphors or similes in the same paragraph or even on the same page.

Clichés are a problem in fiction because they make our writing feel stale. They give readers that feeling of "I've heard this before." That can lead to their attention wandering, and some clichés can even be annoying to readers.

Cut all clichés and find a more interesting way to say what you're trying to say. Or put a twist on a cliché that makes it surprising and fresh again.

(If you're not sure whether what you've written is a cliché or not, there's a great list at http://clichesite.com.)

FLOWERY ABSTRACTIONS

When we move on to the chapter on good description, we're going to talk about preferring the specific to the general. The fraternal twin of that point is that we should also prefer clear, concrete details to flowery, abstract ones.

Flowery abstractions happen when we're trying to find an innovative way to describe something that doesn't need to be described in a fresh way.

For example, write *blue eyes* not *sapphire pools.* Have you ever met anyone who actually thinks of someone else's—or worse, their own—eyes as sapphire pools? (It is alright, however, to describe her eye color as sapphire because that's a specific shade of blue.)

Another example of flowery writing would be referring to a character's hair as *locks* or *tresses.*

Her raven locks spilled down her back.

Part of writing good description is learning when to enhance a description and when to leave it plain. Flowery descriptions aren't a good idea because they make it feel like we're trying too hard.

AN ABUNDANCE OF ADVERBS AND ADJECTIVES

An adjective is a word used to modify or describe a noun or pronoun. They often explain which kind, which one, or how many.

Wise grandfather
Perfect shot
Three dogs
Very happy
Cowardly lion

An adverb does the same thing for verbs, adjectives, or other adverbs. They often answer the questions *how? when?* or *where?*

Come by *tomorrow*
Drive *carefully*
Sit up *straight*

Some, but not all, adjectives and adverbs end in –ly.

Adverbs and adjectives can contribute to purple prose when you use them to try to modify everything or when you use them to modify something that doesn't need modification.

I've bolded the adverbs and adjectives in this passage.

Elodie dove into the **wet** water, and kicked **with both legs** for the **lake** bottom **below** her. **Grimy** silt and **green**, **floating** algae made it **nearly** impossible to see past her **outstretched** fingertips. She **blindly** groped

through the **squishy** sludge. If she didn't find the **fairy**
amulet soon, she'd need to go up **to the surface** for air.

While this isn't a bad passage, it's flabby because of their overuse.
For example, water is by nature wet, so we don't need to add an adjective to tell the reader it's wet. We've already let the reader know
that Elodie can't see past the ends of her fingers, so we don't need to
also tell them she *blindly* groped. And have you ever known sludge
to be anything but squishy?

Here's one way to eliminate the purple elements and tighten up
the passage.

> Elodie dove into the water and kicked for the bottom. Silt
> and floating algae made it impossible to see past her out-
> stretched fingertips. She groped through the sludge. It
> squished between her fingers and coated her hands. If she
> didn't find the amulet soon, she'd need to go up for air.

Perhaps you would have left in a few other adjectives and adverbs. That's fine. What we choose to keep and what we choose to
take out is part of what distinguishes our individual voices. The
point is that not everything needs to be described using an adjective
or an adverb.

ARE ADJECTIVES AND ADVERBS ALWAYS EVIL?

Of course not!

Sometimes an adverb or adjective is necessary and useful. Along
with the purple prose check, ask yourselves these questions to help
decide when to delete or replace your adjectives and adverbs and
when to leave them.

Can I replace this adjective or adverb with a stronger noun or verb?

> *Original:* She said softly.
> *Improved:* She whispered.

> *Original:* He walked heavily.
> *Improved*: He lumbered.

Does this adjective or adverb add something to the meaning?

> *Original:* He yelled loudly.
> *Improved:* He yelled.

You can't yell softly. Volume is inherent in the meaning of the word *yell* in the same way that *wet* is inherent in the meaning of the word *water* in our purple prose example. However, writing *murky water* or *clear water* would add something to the meaning.

> *Original:* She whispered softly.
> *Improved:* She whispered.
> *Also Okay:* She whispered conspiratorially.

Can you put what you're trying to describe via the adjective or adverb into action instead?

Let me continue with the example I just used to illustrate this point.

> *Original:* "You know how he is," she whispered.
> *With Adverb:* "You know how he is," she whispered con-
> spiratorially.

But can you see a way to show this?

Showing: She brought her hand up beside her mouth as if hiding her words from everyone but me. "You know how he is."

I'll give you one more example.

Original: The strong, loud wind whipped around the building.
Improved: The wind rattled the windows.

In this case, it would be easy to think we're okay because *whipped* is a strong verb, but we have an adjective modifying *wind*, not an adverb modifying *whipped*. Consequently, what we need to look for is a more vivid way to show the strength and volume of the wind through action.

One of the most commonly taught guidelines in writing is *show, don't tell*. In the first example, we tell the reader about the strong, loud wind. In the second example, we show them. If you're not sure what I mean by showing and telling, check out Appendix A.

CHAPTER FIVE

Characteristics of a Good Description

SINCE WE'VE BRIEFLY LOOKED AT WHAT makes a bad description, it's time to flip it around and create a checklist of the characteristics of good description. (Many of these concepts are similar, but I find it helps solidify an idea in our mind if we look at it from different angles.)

A GOOD DESCRIPTION IS SPECIFIC

We can easily make the mistake of thinking we've covered the description base in our fiction by writing something generic about the setting. Then we don't understand why readers find our descriptions flat and boring, and why we're getting feedback that our description slows the book down.

Let's look at an example.

Trees spread out before her across the length of the horizon.

I've described what the character sees in front of her, but I've done it in a general way. General = boring. Specific = interesting.

Are these orange and lemon trees in blossom? Oak and maple trees whose leaves have flamed into lipstick reds and crayon oranges? Pine trees whose cones will be exactly what she needs to light a fire?

Carrie Underwood's song "Before He Cheats" is an excellent example of how specific details can bring a storyline to life. How boring would it have been if she simply hit his car with a bat rather than smashing in both his headlights (not just one) with a Louisville Slugger? We learn about the girlfriend's character through those details. We also learn about her cheating boyfriend through the details used to describe him and his car. Even if you don't like country music, listen to this song on YouTube and see how the details are the key to its success.

Obviously, specificity can be overdone. Specific details used well ground your reader in the setting and bring it to life. Naming everything would mean that nothing stands out, so seek balance. Writing, like life, should rarely be all or nothing.

A GOOD DESCRIPTION USES THE FIVE SENSES (NOT JUST SIGHT)

Few things make a setting stick with a reader more than use of all five senses.

We could build on our tree example by adding scent and touch.

> Orange and lemon trees, limbs sagging with fruit, spread out across the length of the horizon. Wafts of fermented citrus made her nose tingle even though she was still a quarter mile away.

Because each sense comes with its own unique strengths and challenges, I'll look at each sense independently in later chapters. What's important to remember for now is that we don't need to use each of the five senses in each passage of description (or even on every page). Like with specificity, we want to find balance so we don't burn the reader out.

A GOOD DESCRIPTION ALLOWS LESS TO BE MORE

Over-describing something doesn't make for a good description (it could actually be included as another red flag for purple prose). When it comes to description, we want to use a couple strong details rather than paragraphs or pages describing everything in excruciating detail.

> She was skinny, and had dyed blonde hair, blue eyes, and a long, hooked nose like the goblins in Harry Potter. It doesn't fit with the rest of her, which has clearly been tucked and Botoxed so that the doctor who delivered her wouldn't recognize anything. I can't imagine why she'd leave a nose like that unless she ran out of money. She'd be almost pretty without that nose…in a creation-of-Dr.-Frankenstein kind of way.
>
> Her dark grey power suit hugs her curves and shows a little too much cleavage to be professional, along with showing the line where her fake tan stops. A gold charm bracelet peaks from beneath her sleeve and jingles as she pokes the keyboard.
>
> She taps her high-heeled foot and looks down at me over the top of the square, black-rimmed, designer glasses perched on top of that nose. "Can I help you?"

We've left the reader with no doubt about what this character looks like, but they're not going to remember all of this. And if we describe every character in this much detail, it will quickly start to blend together in the reader's mind. We'd be better to give them the details that best capture the character. (Remembering, of course, that what details we choose to show will depend on our story, and also on the genre we're writing in.)

Here's one way we might tighten up this passage:

> She has dyed blonde hair, blue eyes, and a long, hooked nose like the goblins in Harry Potter. It doesn't fit with the rest of her, which has clearly been tucked and Botoxed so that the doctor who delivered her wouldn't recognize anything. I can't imagine why she'd leave a nose like that unless she ran out of money. Without it she'd be almost pretty…in a creation-of-Dr.-Frankenstein kind of way.
>
> She looks down at me over the top of the black-rimmed glasses perched on the top of that nose. "Can I help you?"

We still get the same impression of a woman trying too hard and just missing the mark, but because we've focused on *that nose*, the reader will remember her. We can trust their imaginations to fill in the rest of the less important details.

When in doubt, stick to the rule of three. Give three details, then move on.

A GOOD DESCRIPTION SHOWS RATHER THAN TELLS

Showing is essential to strong description because it helps us be specific and bring the experience to life on the page. (If you're not sure what I mean by showing rather than telling, check out Appendix A.)

I'll give you a quick example.

Telling: He was ugly and deformed.

Showing: The skin on the right side of his face seemed to melt down like candle wax, and as he limped toward her, one leg dragged behind.

Just remember that telling isn't always a bad thing. It's a tool like showing and we need to know how to use it strategically. Description, though, usually isn't the place for it.

CHAPTER SIX

The Five Senses In Fiction

ONE THING WE NEED TO DO TO MAKE our fiction come alive is use the five senses. We're going to cover each sense in depth over the next five chapters, but when we first start trying to do that, it's easy to accidentally violate the *show, don't tell* principle through words like *saw, smelled, tasted, felt,* and *heard.* Yet, if we simply do a search for those words and cut them out, we can end up losing important elements of our voice as well.

We need to find the balance. When we do a search for those words in our second (or third or fourth) draft, how can we know when to revise and when to leave them in?

This is something I talk about in detail in my *Busy Writer's Guide* on *Showing and Telling in Fiction,* but because it's such an important element of using the five senses in description, I hope you'll forgive me for repeating some of it here. I've also added some new material to it, so it won't be simply a straight refresher.

If you haven't read *Showing and Telling in Fiction* yet, then this might be brand new ground for you. (And if you're not sure what I even mean by showing and telling, remember that I've explain it in Appendix A.)

Let's start with a simple example.

> *Telling*: Pat heard a gunshot in the distance.

> *Showing*: A gunshot echoed over the treetops.

In the telling version, we've taken a step back, making ourselves more distant from the story. I'm telling you what happened, but I'm not letting you experience it. In the showing version, we're standing beside Pat (or we're inside his head), and so we experience the sound of the gunshot along with him. This is where point of view and showing vs. telling intersect. If the viewpoint character doesn't experience something, then it can't appear on the page.

In other words, you don't need to tell us he heard a gunshot. Unless Pat is deaf, we know he heard the gunshot. You need to let us hear the gunshot along with him.

Remember our example about the fruit trees in the previous chapter? I'm going to play off of that to give you an example using sight and smell.

> *Telling*: Emily saw orange and lemon trees on the horizon line, and the air smelled like spoiled fruit.

Not bad, right? You get an idea of where Emily is, and you know it smells bad. But we can bring it alive by bringing it closer.

> *Showing*: Orange and lemon trees, limbs sagging with fruit, spread out across the length of the horizon. Wafts of fermented citrus made her nose tingle even though she was still a quarter mile away.

By taking away *saw* and *smelled*, we're forced to think about vivid details that can bring a scene to life.

But does that mean it's always wrong to use the words *saw*, *smelled*, *tasted*, *felt*, and *heard*?

When it comes to writing, I don't like to talk about "rules" because I find writers get all bent out of shape and suddenly they start wanting to be rule breakers or they talk about how rules should be broken, etc., etc. We get so caught up in the terminology that the focus shifts from what it should be on—making our writing the best it can be.

So as you go through this entire book, I want you to think of these items as guidelines or best practices. These are the things that should be done 99% of the time. There are exceptions, but these things are how we should normally act for the best results.

Thinking about all of this as best-practice guidelines frees us up to look at these as ways we can make our writing better, rather than thinking about them like rules, which so many writers seem to think they need to violate if they want to be innovative.

If you're going to stray from these guidelines, make sure that you're getting a bigger improvement from it than you'll be losing in what it costs you because violating these guidelines will cost you something. Don't assume that you or your book are the exception, the one that doesn't need to follow these guidelines. You're probably not the exception. Don't try to be innovative in the craft of writing. Be innovative in your story itself and in your characters and in the emotions.

There are three times in particular when it's okay to use the words *saw*, *smelled*, *heard*, *felt*, or *tasted*.

In Similes

A simile is a figure of speech that compares two unlike things that resemble each other in some way, often using the words *like* or *as*.

I'll give you some examples.

> I was in a hospital bed when I regained consciousness. An IV needled poked from the delicate skin on the back of my hand, and I **felt** like a piece of raw meat pounded flat (from my suspense short story "A Purple Elephant" in *Frozen*).

> The spoon clinked against the inside of the cup, and the white powder dissolved into the dark depths of her tea. She raised the cup to her nose and drew in the steam. It **smelled** like fenugreek and honey (from my historical fantasy *Cursed Wishes*, releasing early 2017).

> She licked her lips. Her dry mouth **tasted** like she'd eaten coal and her eyelids were unusually heavy (from my historical fantasy *Cursed Wishes*).

> My thoughts **felt** like a kite caught in a strong wind, tattered and uncontrollable—it was impossible to concentrate.

What I want you to notice is that you need the words *smelled*, *tasted*, and *felt* in the above examples or you can't write the simile (at least not without replacing them with a boring state-of-being verb like *were* or *was*).

All of these examples could have been written without the simile, and thus kept strictly to showing, but they would have lost their power.

I'll show you what I mean. Here's another example. The man has slipped off the edge of a cliff, and the woman is hanging onto his hand, trying to pull him back up.

He dangled above the hundred-foot drop—the same drop where we'd double bungee jumped a year before and joked about who'd inherit our meager savings if the cord broke. My arm felt like a worn bungee cord now, stretched too thin and ready to snap. I wasn't going to be able to hang on much longer.

This time I'll strip it of the simile to make it strictly show.

He dangled above the hundred-foot drop—the same drop where we'd double bungee jumped a year before and joked about who'd inherit our meager savings if the cord broke. My shoulder ached, and my arm trembled. I wasn't going to be able to hang on much longer.

There are a lot of other ways that paragraph could have been written, but without the simile, it feels different. You don't get the same visual. In some situations we might prefer the straight version over the one with the metaphor, but we have the option to use a metaphor even though it employs a sense word.

When the Narrator Is Saying Something About the Thing Sensed

This is a distinction that's often missed. There's a difference between listing that something was sensed and making an assumption or observation about the sense. One is telling. The other is good internal dialogue (a.k.a. the character thinking).

Listing: Marianne heard him call her name.

Observing: He called her name and Marianne stopped. She'd heard him say her name a thousand times before—all the times he'd said *I love you*, all the times he'd used it as a weapon when they fought, all the times he'd called out for her when he came home from work—but it'd never sound-ed like this before. Empty and clinical. The same way she'd expect to hear her name called in a doctor's office.

In More Distant POV

If you're writing in omniscient POV or in a very distant third-person POV, then you can include these words because those narrative styles allow it. I'm not saying you *should*. I'm saying you *can*. Technically, omniscient POV is all telling because the narrator isn't a single character. The narrator is someone all-knowing who stands outside of the story.

If you're writing in omniscient POV, make sure you don't use those five-senses words as a crutch. To do omniscient well, you need an even more vibrant voice and an even better eye for key details than when you write in some other POV because the narrative voice is part of the draw.

CHAPTER SEVEN

Helping Readers See Your World

ACCORDING TO *BRAIN RULES* BY JOHN Medina, a molecular biologist, when it comes to memory, the human brain has what's called a pictorial superiority effect (PSE). Vision is our dominant sense and takes up 50 percent of our brain's resources. People will remember only 10 percent of what they're taught if it's presented orally, but they'll remember 65 percent if that information is accompanied by a picture. (Written words are more effective than lectures but less effective than images.) Because of PSE, when we read, our brains automatically try to visualize what the words are telling us.[1]

To put this another way, the sense of sight is essential to include when we're adding description to our novels. Our readers' brains are going to try to picture what's happening, and the easier we can make that for them, the more engrossed they'll become in the story.

---

[1] John Medina, *Brain Rules: 12 Principles for Surviving and Thriving at Work, Home, and School* (Pear Press, 2009), 233-235.

This doesn't mean including the sense of sight comes without challenges however.

AVOIDING THE TOM BOMBADIL PROBLEM

It took me three tries to finish Tolkien's *The Fellowship of the Ring*. I stalled out the first two times in the same place—at the house of Tom Bombadil. I tried to slog through all the description, but my attention would slip, I'd set the book down, and something more interesting would steal its place. On the third try, I skipped that section and sailed through the rest of the series.

Most readers aren't going to be so determined to read our book, and the biggest trap when it comes to over-describing is the sense of sight. And that's logical. It's the sense we use the most, and it's the sense we need to include the most so the reader gets a solid grasp of our setting.

But how do we include enough sight details without creating the Tom Bombadil problem?

ALLOW YOUR CHARACTER TO PUT THEIR OWN TWIST ON IT

We looked at this earlier. Everything needs to be said the way our viewpoint character would. What would our viewpoint character notice? How would they describe it?

Now take it bigger.

Is our character an optimist or do we want to show her in a good mood? Have her notice the one point of beauty in an otherwise ugly item.

Want to show the character arc? How does what they notice about a particular object change over the course of the story?

In a romantic suspense I'm working on, the main character is given a cactus at the beginning of the book. It's one of many flower arrangements and plants she takes home from the funeral after the death of a loved one. She hates the cactus. She thinks it's ugly. It's all knobby and covered in quills.

But as the book continues, that cactus is the only plant she doesn't accidentally kill because it's naturally resilient. In fact, it eventually blossoms with a beautiful candy apple red flower. How she feels about that cactus changes over the course of the book and reflects how her opinion of her own life changes.

PUT WHAT YOUR CHARACTER SEES INTO MOTION

Unlike the other senses, sight often takes more than a single detail to give us a vivid picture, especially if the setting or character we're describing is important. While adding action (or at least a feeling of motion) won't fix a giant info dump, it can ensure longer descriptions still have forward momentum.

Let me show you an example:

> The wind whipped her black hair around her face, each strand coming alive like Medusa's snakes, and her eyes were squished shut as if she was the one afraid of being turned to stone.

Many times we can combine this technique with a metaphor or simile the way I did above. I'll be talking more about figures of speech in Chapter Twelve.

You see many best-selling authors using this description-in-action technique. Suzanne Collins puts description into action in *The Hunger Games* where she likens Rue to a bird poised to take flight.

N. K. Jemisin uses this technique when she describes the god Nahadoth in her Hugo and Nebula-nominated novel *The Hundred Thousand Kingdoms*. Each element of Nahadoth that she describes—from his face to his hair to his cloak—is put into motion, wavering like the moon or wafting like smoke.

You can see another example of this in Douglas Adams' *Hitchhiker's Guide to the Galaxy*, but Adams puts a slightly different twist on it by giving the impression of action using inaction. Ford Prefect doesn't blink enough, and the narrator's eyes want to water on his behalf (which makes the reader's eyes want to water as well). Ford's skin seems to be pulled back from the center of his face. Those are both technically static descriptions, but his unblinking eyes elicit a reaction in the narrator (and in the reader) and the word *pulled* makes it feel like his skin is being actively stretched and might snap at any moment. The inaction was still described using an active verb. (I'll give you another example of this in a second.)

Sometimes we won't be able to put the item itself into motion, but we can integrate it into action by a character.

Here's a static description:

> A rickety-looking chair sat in the corner of the room. I walked over and took a seat.

In that example, the chair is described separate from the action. But we could interweave it with the action instead.

Take a look:

> I walked over and flopped down into the rickety-looking chair in the corner of the room.

The chair isn't in motion any more than it was in the first example, but we've made it a part of the character's action rather than stopping the action dead for a line of static description.

We could also describe the chair using an active, emotionally-charged verb like we saw in the example from *Hitchhiker's Guide to the Galaxy*. This technique hints at action even when none is present.

Here are a couple options for our rickety chair:

> A rickety-looking chair lurked in the corner of the room.

> A rickety-looking chair hunched in the corner of the room.

Again, the chair still isn't moving, but we've given it more life by adding an interpretation by the viewpoint character of *how* it's sitting in that corner.

BREAK EXPECTATIONS BY PLAYING WITH OPPOSITES

One of the biggest challenges with sight descriptions is to avoid simply conforming to expectations. If we give the reader exactly what they're expecting, then the description will feel flat and boring.

For example, say we have a bouquet of flowers. The expectation is that we'll describe the soft petals, rich fragrance, vibrant colors, or long stems. Because that's what the reader expects, it doesn't matter how well-written our description is. It will always feel like something they've heard before.

An easy way to shake things up and make sure the reader pays attention is to seek the opposite of what's expected. Instead of describing how beautiful a bouquet of flowers is, find something ugly to describe about it. Instead of describing how peaceful a sunset makes our character feel, find a reason to make that sunset stressful to them. Instead of describing how creepy and frightening the giant spider in our character's new home is, instead find a way to describe the beautiful and comforting aspects of that spider.

So before we describe something our character sees, we should ask how this thing is usually described and see if we can describe it in an opposite (and therefore fresh) way.

Another way we can play with expectations is to have our viewpoint character describe how other people see something, and then contrast that with how the viewpoint character sees it differently.

> When he stood on stage, the crowds saw their picture-perfect senator, the next Kennedy or Clinton. A head taller than every man around him, strong jaw, touch of grey at his temples, and a smile that could have sold toothpaste to people without teeth. But all she saw were the hands that left bruises in places no one else could see.

Orson Scott Card uses this technique in *Ender's Game* in the description of Peter, Ender's older brother. The adults only seem to see how handsome Peter is. What Ender notices about Peter isn't his physical looks but rather the changing expressions on his face, harbingers of pain for Ender.

Closely related to this is describing the way a person once was with how they are now—how they've changed since the viewpoint character saw them last.

Our first introduction to King Robert Baratheon in *Game of Thrones* by George R. R. Martin comes through Ned Stark's eyes—eyes that remember the king in his prime, strong and smelling of blood and leather. The Robert who comes to Winterfell after so many years is fat and smells of perfume instead. Had Martin only described King Robert as he presently was, we'd have had no idea of how far he'd fallen. It's the contrast, the opposites, that make the description so powerful and memorable.

Another way to play with opposites is to give a single character two qualities that seem to contradict each other. It's interesting because it keeps the reader wondering which is the truth and which is the lie.

An excellent example of this shows up in *Nineteen Eighty-Four* by George Orwell. The character of Julia wears a sash for the Junior Anti-Sex League, but she's tied it tightly enough to show off her shapely hips.

EXPLOIT THE SCOPE OF WHAT OUR EYES CAN TAKE IN

When we write about what characters see, we often default to describing size and color, but size and color aren't the only visual elements our eyes can take in. They also take in shapes, textures, patterns, depth, shadows, and even optical illusions. What our character sees on first glance might not be what's actually there once they take a closer look. If a description is feeling flat, see if you can forego the regular descriptions of size and color and bring it to life through other visual elements instead.

USE GENDER DIFFERENCES

This point overlaps a bit with the previous one in that studies have found clear gender differences in what people notice first. As writers, we can use this to our advantage to make visual descriptions belonging to our male viewpoint characters feels distinctive from visual descriptions belonging to our female viewpoint characters.

Men tend to notice first the size of things, how fast something is moving, body posture, and women's body shapes (even if they don't find them attractive). And when they're in the middle of a task, they essentially get tunnel vision. This means that if your male viewpoint character is working on something, he'll only notice (and describe) elements relevant to that task.

Women, on the other hand, will first notice facial expressions, colors, and textures. They're also more likely to notice things outside of the task they're working on.

This doesn't mean that men won't notice colors or women won't notice size. It just means that these wouldn't likely be the first thing they notice.

FOCUS ON "THE ONE" RATHER THAN ON "THE MANY"

Remember back in Chapter Five where we talked about giving specific details rather than general ones? When it comes to the sense of sight, this extends further than saying *oak tree* rather than *tree*. Whenever possible, we should focus on describing "the one" rather than "the many."

The best way I can explain this to you is by giving you an example. Say we have a character named Jeanette who's out for a walk. I write this…

A pack of dogs charged toward Jeanette.

What do you see based on that? Are these hellhounds coming to kidnap her? Starving feral dogs? Or is she a breeder who took her litter of Lab puppies out for a run and now all twelve of them are preparing to launch their tiny, furry bodies at her?

Context would help the reader figure out what they're supposed to imagine, but even if this is a fantasy, you'd have a hard time picturing what's happening if all I wrote was…

A pack of hellhounds charged toward Jeanette.

The problem with these examples is humans struggle to imagine groups of things. It's due to the way our eyes are structured.

Human beings have a single fovea in each eye. The fovea is basically the spot in our eye with the highest resolution (in other words, the spot that creates the clearest picture), and it only covers the middle 40 degrees of our vision. The greatest concentration of our eyes' cones (the part responsible for color vision) only covers about 10 degrees of that.

So we're able to focus clearly on what's in front of us, but what's off to the sides is fuzzier. We're aware it's there, but we can't make out the details clearly if we're not looking directly at it.

In other words, if a group of anything came at us in real life, we wouldn't be able to focus on all of it at once. We'd focus on one member of the group at a time, and our brains would extrapolate about the rest of the group from that member. Our brains are hardwired to work with eyes that excel at focusing on a single object at a time.

Because of this, when we're writing, even if we want to describe a large group, we should begin by describing one member of that group.

> The lead hellhound had the height and girth of a bull bred for the arenas. Its black fur stuck up in clumps, as if cemented together with blood and sweat. Strings of saliva stretched from its fangs, and it turned its crimson eyes on her. A long howl ripped through the still air, and it charged, the rest of the pack close on its heels.

Now that we know what one member looks like, we'll fill in the blanks about the others, but the experience will be a vivid and living one for us.

GIVE ORDER TO THE DESCRIPTION

On so many levels, fiction needs to imitate life, sometimes in very subtle ways. As writers, there are certain things we can do to make our writing more immersive for the reader. When a reader feels like the text is clunky or when a reader doesn't connect to a description, sometimes the problem is as simple as the description being out of order.

Think about how we observe things in life.

If we're looking at a person for the first time, we don't look at their eyes and then their feet and then their hair and then their legs. We usually start at the top and work our way down, start at the bottom and work our way up, or we focus on one feature or area (for example, the person's face) and become so distracted by it that we don't notice anything else about them.

When we're writing a description, we should also write it in the same logical progression. Your female main character meets her future love interest and she notices his eyes, then his broad shoulders, then his bicycler's thighs. She doesn't notice his eyes, then his thighs, then his shoulders.

The same principle holds true for broader descriptions. Your character might notice things in the distance and then pan closer until they start paying attention to what's right in front of them. They might go in the opposite direction, noticing what's close first and then what's farther away. What they won't do is notice what's close, what's far, and then what's in the middle. That's not the way our brain naturally processes information.

Let's look again at my description of the hellhound pack leader.

> The lead hellhound had the height and girth of a bull bred for the arenas. Its black fur stuck up in clumps, as if cemented together with blood and sweat. Strings of saliva

stretched from its fangs, and it turned its crimson eyes on her.

With each detail, I've narrowed the focus. I start with the general idea of size, then the fur that covers the whole body, and finally I focused in on the face. Broad to narrow.

If your sight descriptions are feeling off balance and you're struggling to identify why, check your order. The solution might be as simple as rearranging a couple of sentences.

CHAPTER EIGHT

Using Sound to Make Your Novel Stand Out in a Sea of Noise

NEXT TO SIGHT, SOUND IS THE MOST commonly used sense in life and in fiction. It's pervasive in a way that few other senses are. You can close your eyes. You can plug your nose. But for those of us who have normal hearing, we can never fully escape sound. Even when the outside world is cut off, we can still hear our own breathing, our own heartbeat.

For us as writers, this creates an incredibly interesting interplay between sound and the lack of sound. If we're limiting ourselves to just naming sounds in our writing, we're missing out on the richness that the sense of sound could bring to our fiction. We're speaking to our readers in a monotone.

In this chapter, I'm going to walk you through some of the ways we can use sound to best effect to enrich our writing.

USE WORDS THAT SOUND LIKE THEIR MEANING FOR AN ECHO

Onomatopoeia is when a word sounds like its definition—hiss, buzz, creak, swish, clatter, yelp. We can use onomatopoetic words in our writing to create the sound in the reader's mind as they read.

The blade scraped across his stubble.

If you've ever listened to a man shave using a razor rather than an electric trimmer, *scrape* imitates the sound you'll hear with each swipe.

You can also use onomatopoetic sounds more directly.

Trina tiptoed across the open alleyway and ducked into the dilapidated house next door. She eased the door shut behind her, and leaned against it. Safe at last.
Creak.
Trina stiffened and slowly lifted her gaze to the ceiling over her head. It might just be the wind. Or they might have found her at last.

Using the onomatopoetic word directly in this way is a controversial technique among writers. Middle grade fantasy author Janice Hardy likes to use this technique in her books, and in defense of it, she argues that it gives a greater sense of immediacy and intimacy (it more closely represents the reader hearing the sound) and also avoids potential point-of-view errors if the viewpoint character doesn't know what made the sound. Pick up one of the books in her *Healing Wars* trilogy if you'd like to see this in action.

She's right in her reasoning. At the same time, not every writer (or reader) likes using onomatopoetic words in this way. If you don't like them, then don't use them. If you do like them, be careful about their use, recognizing that they aren't loved by everyone.

Another poetry technique worth judiciously stealing is the repetition of sounds within words to mimic the sound you're describing. One of the best examples is from the final lines of Tennyson's "Come Down, O Maid."

The moan of doves in immemorial elms
And murmur of innumerable bees.

A morning dove's call at a quiet summer's twilight carries the same long *o* sound as *moan*, and the sequence of *m*'s and *n*'s followed by the *zee* sound in *bees* creates a buzz like a swarm.

Here's another simpler example.

The fly zipped around my head.

The *zzz* sound in *zipped* imitates the annoying sound a buzzing fly makes without actually having to state that it buzzed.

Because most of us vocalize in our minds when we read, onomatopoeic words and phrases help us hear the sound you're describing. (Speed readers are trained to stop this internal vocalization because it slows reading speed, but it's also one of the things that helps make reading so pleasurable.)

Don't overuse this technique. Not everyone likes it. Personally, used frugally at moments when you really need to emphasize a sound, I love it.

PLAY WITH THE EMOTIONAL EFFECTS OF SOUND DEPRIVATION OR SOUNDS WE CAN'T CONTROL

Using the sense of sound effectively in fiction isn't all about the type of sound. Sometimes it's about the lack of sound, the volume, the duration, or whether we have any control over the sound. Beyond this, it's about our character's emotional reaction to the sounds they hear.

When the power goes out in your house at night, do you sleep through it or does the sudden loss of the white noise of the appliances wake you up? Do you find the loss peaceful or, after a while, does the silence become almost oppressive and ominous?

Scientists have studied the effects of sensory deprivation on the human body, and discovered a short period of sensory deprivation, like being underwater, can be relaxing. Over extended periods of time, though, it can lead to hallucinations, decreased memory function, and loss of identity, which is why it's used as "white torture." If you place your character in a situation where they can't hear, they're likely to be disoriented at first, feeling almost like their ears are clogged. If you place them alone for a long period of time somewhere like the wilds of Utah in winter, the silence will begin to play tricks with their mind.

Similarly, if we have the ability to make a sound stop, we're more able to tolerate it than if we have to endure it with no knowledge of when it might end. While our body eventually learns to ignore soft noises like the ticking of a clock in the background, louder noises or noises intended to motivate us to action can't be tuned out in the same way. In my last truck, the parking break broke, but I didn't realize it until I'd set it for a ferry ride, and the warning ding kept going after I released it. I had to drive over an hour with no way to make it stop. The sound never bothered me before, but by the end of that drive, I was tense and irritable and fighting a headache. It wasn't so much the sound itself as it was my loss of control over it that incited my reaction.

When you include a sound in your fiction, consider whether your viewpoint character, or the characters around them, would naturally have an emotional reaction to that sound (or the lack thereof).

LET SOUND SET THE MOOD

They don't call it mood music for nothing. Your choice of sounds can alter the whole feel of a scene, so choose carefully to create the mood you want your reader to feel. If you want to lighten a scene, add a funny or embarrassing sound to a somber or romantic moment.

One of my favorite lines from my co-writer in our historical fantasy is when our female lead's closest friend says to her, "The wind carries the voices of the dead tonight." It described the actual moaning sound of the wind. It also highlighted not only the grief they shared yet couldn't speak of, but their dread and uncertainty over what they'd face the next day.

REMEMBER TO INCLUDE BACKGROUND NOISE

I'm using the term background noise as a sort of catch-all for the daily noises we take for granted. When you watch a movie or a TV show, those sounds are there. Directors make sure to include a horn honking, a dog barking, dishes clattering in the sink, whiny car breaks, laugher from the next table, a clock ticking, and so on. They do it because, if it wasn't there, the setting wouldn't feel real. The same is true for our fiction. Our viewpoint character should be aware of the sounds going on around them.

This extends into our character's interactions with other people as well. What do they notice about the voice of the character they're talking to? Is it gravelly? Surprisingly high or low pitched? Do they speak so softly that our character has to lean in to hear them? Do they have an accent?

If our viewpoint character is stuck next to someone—for example, in a meeting, a movie theater, or a grocery store line—what noise becomes annoying that they wouldn't notice in quarters that aren't so close and extended? Does the person have a whistle when they breathe? Are they a throat-clearer? A sniffler? Are they chewing their gum with their mouth open so our character can hear every pop and squish? Squeaking the damp sole of their running shoe on the tiles of the floor? Clicking their pen?

Little details of sound help bring your setting to life for the reader, something we'll talk about more later. Don't assume that they'll add these on their own. If we don't put them on the page, they won't hear them in their head.

EXTRA TIP

You can also play with the sound of words more indirectly. Certain words aren't onomatopoetic—they aren't even words describing sounds—but they sound right for their meaning.

Stodgy means heavy, dull, uninteresting, or stocky. The word itself gives the impression of a heavyset man moving slowly.

Ooze means to move slowly, often through a small opening, or to exude moisture. It sounds right for its meaning.

When you've finished your early drafts and you're trying to polish your work, ask yourself if you've used the right word, or if you might be able to find a word where the sound matches the meaning to give an added richness to what you've written.

CHAPTER NINE

Using Taste to Make Readers Hungry for More

I N THE LAST TWO CHAPTERS WE LOOKED AT sight and sound. Now we're going to take a bite out of taste (sorry, couldn't help myself) with ways to enhance the flavors in our book.

DECIDE WHEN NAMING A TASTE IS ENOUGH VS. WHEN YOU NEED TO DESCRIBE IT

Some tastes are potent enough and familiar enough that all we need to do is name them. Chocolate chip cookie dough ice cream. A cinnamon-flavored toothpick. Your dentist's latex gloves. Because they're part of our shared experience, describing them doesn't enhance the story at all. Instead, it becomes the kind of excess description we're so often advised to cut.

A foreign taste, though, always needs a description; otherwise, you're just placing an empty word on the page. In my co-written historical fantasy, our male viewpoint character drinks a glass of *kumiss*, fermented mare's milk with an almond aftertaste. Simply dropping in the word *kumiss* wouldn't have heightened your sensory experience at all. In the same way that describing a familiar taste is pointless, so is dropping in a foreign word and expecting the reader to understand it. Now, even though you've likely never tasted *kumiss*, can you imagine the sharp tang, like buttermilk gone bad, and then just as you finish swallowing, the slight sweet nuttiness of almond lingering on your tongue and in the back of your mouth?

(This is actually a perfect example of the confusion I often see in writers who are told both that they need description in their story to bring it to life and also that description slows down their story and they should cut it. The right kind of description doesn't slow the story down at all. Unnecessary description does. Do you see the difference in the two situations above?)

The trick in describing a taste is to do it in a way that doesn't break point of view and end up feeling like author intrusion. For the example I used above from the manuscript Lisa Hall-Wilson and I wrote, we got around this by having our male character crave the flavor of this particular drink as opposed to the wine he'd been offered. When your character is craving a particular food, or savoring it, it's natural for them to think about the flavors the same way we would in those situations.

USE METAPHORS OR OTHER COMPARISONS

Our brains are wired to compare things we don't have experience with to something we do. Taste lends itself well to metaphors or other comparisons. Sometimes you don't need to describe a taste literally to convey its essence.

> The water rolling over her swollen tongue and down her parched throat tasted the way the air smelled after a summer storm.

> The hot pepper tasted like she'd swallowed a mouthful of bumblebees.

> He told stories of fruit that tasted the way rubies look and eggs as big as his head.

We're going to look at metaphors and similes more in a later chapter.

MAKE IT SURPRISING SOMEHOW

You come home from the grocery store with a bag of what appear to be sweet, crunchy grapes only to pop one onto your tongue and get a mouthful of moldiness. Things don't always taste the way we expect.

You can also use other senses to turn expectations upside down. Parmesan cheese smells like stinky feet and cumin smells like body odor, but both of them add a delicious flavor to dishes. And because we eat first with our eyes, when food looks unappetizing, we remember it that much more when it actually tastes good.

USE THE FULL SCOPE OF WHAT WE CAN TASTE AND THEN GO BEYOND IT

The four "basic" tastes are sweet, sour, salty, and bitter. Because those are so common, we tend to default to them when we write.

But the range of tastes and textures we can experience with our tongues is actually much broader.

Scientists now recognize that our tongue also has receptors for L-glutamate as well. This fifth taste is called umami (savory). When you eat something delicious that isn't sweet, sour, salty, or bitter, what you're tasting is umami. Think about it. When you last ate a cheeseburger, it probably wasn't sweet, sour, salty, or bitter. Beef and cheese both contain glutamate. It was umami.

Along with the basic tastes, our tongues can recognize the heat level of a food. This means both whether it's objectively hot like coffee or cold like ice cream and where it falls on the piquancy-coolness scale. Foods that are high in capsaicin (like certain peppers) trick our brains into feeling a burn or a sensation of heat even from foods that aren't objectively hot. Foods that contain menthol (like peppermint) are interpreted by our brains as cool, minty, and fresh, even though they're not actually objectively cold.

When you're describing the flavor of a food, consider which of these elements is involved and find a fresh way to express it.

You can also go beyond simple taste. What's the texture of the food or drink? Gritty? Slimy? Crunchy? Chewy? Bubbly? Often we stop at taste, when texture plays almost as large a role in what we think about a food as does taste. Examples of this are the distinct preference most people exhibit for either smooth or chunky peanut butter or for either pulp-free orange juice or juice with pulp.

DON'T LIMIT YOURSELF TO DESCRIBING TASTE ONLY WHEN YOUR CHARACTER IS EATING OR DRINKING

We experience taste many times during the average day, not just when we're eating or drinking. Vanilla chapstick, the saltiness of sea spray, the metallic tang when we accidentally bite the inside of our cheek, the film on our teeth if we haven't been able to brush, the chalkiness of the paper we hold between our lips because our hands are full, the grit in our mouths after we go running on a dusty road,

When you're trying to add the sense of taste to your story, think outside of the regular limits of meal or snack times. If you're drawing a blank on ideas, keep a notebook with you for a week. Every time you experience a taste, write it down.

CONSIDER THE OUTSIDE FACTORS THAT INFLUENCE OUR PERCEPTION OF TASTE

People who develop a food allergy later in life will talk about how the flavor of the food in question suddenly changed. What once tasted good to them now tastes bad. Our bodies often exhibit a natural aversion to foods that are poisonous or which will cause an allergic reaction.

This opens up new opportunities where the sense of taste is concerned in our stories. Think about your particular plot and how this sixth sense might come into play. For example, do you have a character who's secretly being slowly poisoned? You can lay a subtle clue by having them notice a different taste to a food or drink they normally love.

Our perception of flavors is also influenced by the memories connected to them. When I was seven, I ate tacos for the first time, and I was sick the next day. The two events probably weren't connected, but tacos have never looked appealing to me since. Cancer patients are advised to not eat their favorite foods shortly after treatment for a similar reason. Our brains can't distinguish between nausea caused by the treatment and nausea caused by the food we just ate. We've been created so that we'll avoid eating something that made us ill in the past.

The memories connected to food can be good as well as bad. Every time I eat KFC, I think about my maternal grandmother. When my parents would go away and she'd come to stay overnight with me, she'd always bring KFC as a special treat for us. When my best friend was killed by a drunk driver, she bought me KFC to tempt me to eat something. I have so many memories of her tied to eating KFC that when she's no longer with us, a meal of KFC will be bittersweet. What memories can you tie to food in your book?

It's these nuanced elements that help make a story feel real rather than created.

CHAPTER TEN

How to Make Your Novel Scratch and Sniff

THE TRICK WITH SMELLS IS THAT IF YOU include too many you can burn your reader out the way you deaden your nose if you smell every candle in the Yankee Candle store. (Not that I'm admitting to having done that...)

These techniques can help you make the most of the smells you choose.

DESCRIBE A SMELL WHEN IT'S FRESH

Unless a smell is particularly pungent, we quickly become desensitized to it. Why does this matter? Well, it lets us know when we should describe a scent, and knowing when to describe something and when not to is half the battle.

For example, if your character enters an evergreen forest, that's the time to describe what her surroundings smell like, not a half hour later when she stops to catch her breath. By the time she's been in the trees for half an hour, she won't smell the evergreens, the moist earth, or the bear droppings anymore.

USE SMELL TO ALERT YOUR CHARACTER TO A CHANGE OR TO IMPENDING DANGER

Closely related to introducing scents when they're fresh is using smells to signal a change—for example, a storm building changes the way the air smells.

Smells can also be an excellent way to alert your character to danger or to hint at danger even though your character isn't aware of the potential ramifications of the smell. When I was growing up, we heated our house primarily with a woodstove. I developed the ability to smell when the woodstove was too hot, entering the danger zone, even from across the house. My husband, who didn't grow up with a woodstove, can't smell the difference.

In the past, humans depended on their sense of smell to warn them of danger or of food sources. They could smell mushrooms or strawberries or apple trees growing in the woods. They could smell a fox, a skunk, or a bear without being able to see them.

Although we no longer depend as heavily on our sense of smell, we still retain the ability. Does your character catch a scent that alerts her that she's being followed? Does she later smell that same scent on someone she thought was her friend? Does she smell gas or smoke filling the house in time to escape?

CONNECT THE SMELL TO AN EMOTION

Smell can be one of the most powerful senses in your fiction because of its ability to evoke emotions. You probably associate certain smells with memories, people, or places. I hate the way the dentist office smells like burning hair. The smell comes from the singed protein of teeth being drilled, and I associate that smell with pain. If I'm stressed, the warm scent of a clean dog will calm me down because I associate it with the comfort I find in my Great Dane when I throw my arms around her.

Think about your own life and what smells evoke memories and emotions. Why do they have that effect on you? You don't need to duplicate that precise smell in your fiction (you should find one that belongs organically to your character), but by paying attention to how smells intertwine throughout your life, you can learn how to build them into your stories.

If you're struggling with how to naturally slide in necessary backstory, smell can be your saving grace. As Roni Loren pointed out in her post "How to Dish Out Backstory in Digestible Bites," something needs to trigger a memory in order to introduce backstory. Because of how memories cling to scents, smells work as a perfect trigger.

CHOOSE ONE "SHOWPIECE" SCENT

In Ted Dekker's The Boneman's Daughter, the serial killer is addicted to Noxzema. I think about it every time I wash my face with Noxzema. That's the staying power of giving a single scent a starring role.

This isn't just for fiction writers. For non-fiction writers, you can create the same lasting memory by finding the one key smell to grab your readers. It could be the difference between a forgettable article or chapter in your book and motivating your readers to act. Are you writing a parenting book? What smell defines motherhood for you? How did that smell grow and change with your child? Differ between sickness and health?

Even though you'll have other scents in your book, weaving one key smell throughout, changing it, playing off of it in moments of tension, ties your entire story together and imprints it on your reader's mind. The next time they smell that scent in the world, they'll think of your book.

CONTRAST A GOOD SMELL WITH A BAD ONE

Choosing two antagonistic scents can be done simply to make both smells stand out more than they would on their own, complement a theme, or subtly support what's happening inside your character.

In my co-written historical fantasy, our main male character is torn between the desire to sleep with his new female slave and the desire to obey his new God who forbids it. He commands her to strip off her tunic, and when she does, the scent of sweat and cypress invades his nostrils. The opposing scents mirror the struggle between his opposing desires.

In *The Hunger Games* trilogy, President Snow smells like blood and roses. He uses the roses to cover up the fact that his breath reeks of blood, and this becomes a metaphor in a way for how the beauty and glitz of the capital tries to disguise the repulsiveness of the country's situation. Suzanne Collins could have just had him smell like blood, but the contrast with something as beautiful and symbolic as roses made the smell of blood that much more grotesque. And Katniss is never able to think about roses the same way again.

CHAPTER ELEVEN

Using Touch to Pull Your Reader Into Your Novel

DID YOU KNOW THAT LEPROSY DOESN'T actually make your fingers and toes fall off? What actually happens is the bacteria attack the nerve endings in the body so the sufferer can't feel pain. When they injure themselves, they don't feel it, and this can lead to infection and gangrene before the injured person realizes it and can get treatment. Imagine if they lost their sense of touch entirely.

Touch is the one sense we can't survive without, so if you're not using it in your story, you're missing a key aspect of the human experience.

USE ALL ASPECTS OF TOUCH

Touch is one of the most multi-faceted senses. You can touch and be touched. You can be touched by another living being, by the weather, or by an inanimate object. To convey touch to your readers, think about temperature, moisture, texture, pressure, and intent.

Temperature is about more than hot and cold. It's about hot and cold within context. A cool hand on a feverish forehead soothes. A cool hand in a handshake is often interpreted as a sign of a cold personality. In an old an episode of *Columbo*, a character's cold hands tipped him off to their poor circulation, and that in turn helped him solve the case.

Moisture is about more than wet and dry. A character who steps outside in the first storm that broke the drought and got soaked to the skin is going to feel very differently about the rain than is a character whose car broke down on the side of the road and they had to walk to a gas station because their cell phone couldn't get a signal.

Texture also goes beyond the gritty sand between your toes or the sliminess of separating an egg with your fingers. Writer Lisa Hall-Wilson once wrote a post on how "The Details Make the Story." For one of her earliest attempts at a novel, she wanted to write about a fireman and so she booked a tour of a fire hall. Near the end of the tour, she asked to feel one of the firemen's hands because she needed to know if they were rough like a farmer's or smooth like a mechanic's.

Pressure can show intimacy, a threat, or add humor. At my best friend's funeral, a well-meaning older lady took my hand and squeezed it while she talked to me. The pressure she used normally wouldn't have been a problem except that when she took my hand, the ring I had on twisted, and every time she squeezed, the stone cut into the finger next to it. She interpreted the pain flashing across my face as grief and squeezed harder. It was funny in hindsight. Not so much at the moment.

Intent adds layers. I once read that women don't slap men they're genuinely furious with. They might punch them, knee them in the groin, shove them, or simply walk away, but they won't slap them because a slap says that part of them isn't angry. Part of them secretly knows the man was right or is secretly attracted to him because of what he did. A slap is ambiguous. Think about what your character intends with their touch (even if they're not the viewpoint character), and choose the right type of touch for the situation.

EXPLORE THE NON-PHYSICAL TOUCH

It might seem like an oxymoron to talk about non-physical touch, but every day we're touched by things that we can't actually touch or hold in return. How does the sun feel on your character's skin? Or the wind? Does the air feel different in their lungs on a humid summer day vs. a cold winter night?

OBSERVE (OR BREAK) THE CONTINUUM OF INTIMACY

By its very nature, touch is an intimate sense. You can smell a scent carried on the wind, hear a sound from a mile away, look at stars through a telescope. To touch something, you need to be within arm's reach.

Jenny Hansen had a helpful post on "Using the 12 Stages of Physical Intimacy to Build Tension in Your Fiction." She's graciously allowed me to share part of that post with you to help you understand the continuum of intimacy. If you'd like to read the whole post, you can find it at Writer's in the Storm (http://writersinthestorm.wordpress.com/), a fantastic blog for writers. Jenny also blogs on her own site at http://jennyhansenauthor.wordpress.com/.

The 12 Stages of Physical Intimacy

1. Eye to body – This is the first "summing up" glance where one character notices the height, weight, and dress code of another and registers an "overall impression." A man will never approach a woman without this step, and it's important to get that first glimpse onto the page.

This step is why "the heroine studying herself in the mirror" is considered such a rookie writing mistake. We want to be in one character's head when they see their fellow main character. Even if the glance is between two friends or business associates, this is the first step in building the emotional intimacy between them.

2. Eye to eye – The first step of active interaction between characters. There is a lot of tension to be found in eye contact and writers need to take a moment to get it on the page. Whether it's a menacing stare or a long glance, you need to bring it to your reader. Remember, the *point-of-view* character needs to always be the person in the scene with the most to lose. When you bring up eye contact, make sure you're in that vulnerable character's head.

3. Voice to voice – Once the two characters have met, they must speak. Who speaks first is important, as is what they say. What if one character touches the other before they speak? *Whoa!* Serious tension. It's your story, so I'll let you figure this out, but think about how to get the most mileage from your scenes as you move through this chart.

4. Hand to hand (or arm) – *"Mom, he's touching me!"* Don't you remember how invasive you found the slightest look or touch from your siblings during a fight? My brother standing at the door of my room staring or putting a fingertip over "the line" and touching me were a *big deal* when we were at war. It wasn't about the touch; it was about crossing my boundary. Remember this when you write and be purposeful in your touching. Push boundaries when it helps your story.

5. Arm to shoulder – Ah...*it's the old yawn and drop the arm around the girl move.* Why is this a Classic? It's because this is serious intimacy. Up close and able to kiss or smell. This is a gateway move to more intimacy.

I HATE it when someone I don't know well puts their arm around me. Why? Because it's intimate and invasive. But if I know them or feel close to them, it's loving and welcome. It's all about boundaries. How wide are your character's boundaries? Why? How quickly does your character relax those boundaries? Again, *why?* These are important questions for you to answer.

6. Arm to waist, or back – *Oooh...the hand on the small of the back to guide a woman through the room.* It melts me every time my guy does this.

Why is this so romantic? Because a warm hand against the small of the back sends the message to the woman and the rest of the room that this man is allowed to touch her, right above her bottom. There is physical comfort between these two people and they are engaging in non-verbal behavior that's nearly always sexual.

7. Mouth to mouth – Have you ever wondered why a kiss is so intimate? You've moved though half the intimacy chart with this one move. Depending on how the kiss progresses, several more intimacy levels may be skipped.

Why do so many romance authors spend time and tension on the kiss, breaking it off or prolonging it? *Because it works!* Kissing creates tension in the pages of your novel, if you do it right, and keeps your readers fanning themselves and turning your pages to see when your characters are going to do it *again.*

8. Hand to head – Perhaps your first kiss back at Step 7 was a lip-lock, possibly including some stroking of the back. Sexy and intimate, but not a "skip-a-level" moment. What about when a man holds a woman's face or vice-versa? What about when the yanking of hair ensues? It's hot because it's extraordinarily intimate to touch a person's head or face.

Use this in your books. The back of a fingertip along someone's cheek and down their neck...is it good, as in hero and heroine? Or evil, as in villain, heroine? You are the creator of your world, be it loving or creepy.

9. Hand to body – This step moves the couple into the beginnings of foreplay. This is a key place to break your couple apart, have deep emotional issues surface, or just to collide your internal and external conflict. You haven't reached the "point of no return" yet, so break the intimacy up a bit. Throw your characters up a tree and shoot at them...it's a nice gift for your readers.

10. Mouth to breast – I always told my baby sister, "No matter what, keep your shirt on until you're *really* sure you want to sleep with a guy."

A woman can still turn back at this point, as can a man, but there's likely to be some stomped feelings on both sides if she does. That's not why I told her to stay clothed. Most women excrete the bonding hormone oxytocin, the "love hormone," when they have skin to skin contact. Why bond with some schmuck if it could have been avoided by just keeping your shirt on?

11. Hand to genitals – We're pretty much at the point of no return at this stage. If somebody changes their mind, labels like "tease" are likely to be assigned and major conflict will ensue. I love the idea of having the external conflict be the *coitus interruptus*. There's some major mileage to be gained from messing with your characters in these final stages.

12. Genitals to genitals – *He shoots, he scores!* You're at the sex act and your characters will commit violence if you interrupt now.

It's nice to decide *in advance* what you want from The Big Sexy. You've made your readers pant for this step throughout the journey, dragging them through ALL the other stages to get here. It is up to you whether this is the payoff, as it is in many romance novels, or if it's just a step to something else in your story.

The entire point to this chart is to get the most from your characters' intimacy. Being deliberate in your steps will pay off big in your stories.

Thank you again to Jenny for allowing me to share that.

Jenny points out that skipping over any of the stages of intimacy causes conflict. Drawing out these stages amps up the tension as your readers hold their breath to see when your characters will reach the next milestone. You can observe or break the order of the touch levels on this scale depending on what emotional effect you want to have on your reader.

Jenny also notes that the stages of physical intimacy speak to boundaries. Personal space boundaries vary by individual, by gender, and by age, but they also vary by culture. In North America, you don't kiss an almost perfect stranger on the cheeks in either greeting or farewell. In other cultures, straight men kiss on the lips in greeting. You can add richness to your story by having touch interact with personal boundaries and cultural norms.

CONSIDER HOW YOUR CHARACTER WILL INTERPRET IT

The most important thing for touch, though, is to know how your character will interpret it. A woman whose love language is physical affection will interpret a hug differently than will a woman who was sexually abused as a child. How will a germaphobe handle touch? What about an aging musician whose fingers are going numb? Like everything else, touch needs to be filtered through your character and given their unique spin.

CHAPTER TWELVE

Metaphors and Similes

METAPHORS AND SIMILES ARE ONE OF the keys to memorable stories because they create images that tap into our emotions. They stick in our minds because they give us something tangible to hang on to.

A simile uses *like* or *as* to compare two different things.

A metaphor goes a step deeper. Instead of saying something is *like* something else, they say something *is* a different thing.

Unfortunately, metaphors and similes don't inherently help our book. Flat ones are forgettable. We have to make them memorable.

HOW TO CREATE MEMORABLE FIGURES OF SPEECH

Make Them Fresh and Unexpected

George Orwell advised, "Never use a metaphor, simile, or other figure of speech which you are used to seeing in print." His point was that if you've seen it in other books before, it's no longer fresh. It might even be verging on clichéd.

The best metaphors and similes stick in people's minds because they don't remember ever hearing them before.

Let's look at an example.

Say we have an angry character. We could choose an overused simile such as *her voice was cold as ice*. But here's one fresher way we could write this.

Her voice would have frozen a lava flow.

Not only is this metaphor fresh, but it tells us about the level of her anger and creates a certain tone. This woman isn't just a little bit angry. She's furious.

We can be playful with this as well. Instead of describing a new acquaintance's hair as *black as coal* (a stale simile), our viewpoint character could think something like...

Her hair was black as my ex-husband's heart.

Maybe we don't learn more about the new character's hair color, but we sure learn a lot about our viewpoint character's relationship with and opinion of her former spouse.

Use Them to Enhance Our Understanding of the Familiar

Oftentimes, we'll use a metaphor or simile to describe something every reader will be familiar with. These figures of speech are in the most danger of running into clichéd territory.

In this situation, we have to use our simile or metaphor to help our reader understand what we're describing in a new way. We want them to have the gut reaction of "Yes, that's exactly how it feels. She just put into words something I've known all along but haven't been able to articulate."

> The fear in my chest is tight and heavy and sharp, like I've had the wind knocked out of me.

> I suspect a few people are saying "Wait! You're naming emotions. Isn't that telling?" Well...yes. And that, my friend, is why I talk about guidelines rather than rules. Telling isn't always bad. We have to know when it use it strategically—like in a meaningful figure of speech.

Not every enhance-the-familiar figure of speech will name an emotion.

Here's how Daniel Swenson describes his main character's medical examination in *The Farthest City*.

> She was second to last when her turn came. Doctors worked her over like she was a stray dog. She was stripped, shaved, sprayed, injected, swabbed, probed, and thoroughly humiliated.

Many of us have been in a medical situation where the doctors are trying to discover what's wrong with us (or a loved one) or to discover if there is something wrong. When I read this, likening it to how a stray dog is treated, I had the moment of "Exactly!"

Use Them to Help Us Experience the Unfamiliar

If you're writing about something your reader will likely have no experience with, choose a simile that will let them equate it with something they'll know.

In *The Help*, Minnie, a black maid, bursts into the bathroom to help her sick employer. Celia lies on the floor, covered in blood after miscarrying her baby. Kathryn Stockett likens the smell of the baby to hamburger thawing on the counter.

A miscarried baby is a situation very few of us will have experienced, so Stockett associated something unfamiliar with something familiar, allowing us to play an intimate part in a foreign experience. We no longer have to have personal experience with a miscarried child to know what it smells like.

MISTAKES WE CAN MAKE WITH FIGURES OF SPEECH

Now that we've looked at the keys to making our metaphors and similes memorable, we need to look at the biggest gaffes we can accidentally make when trying to write a metaphor or simile. It's one thing to make these fumbles if you're trying to write corny humor. It's an entirely different thing to make them accidentally. (It's the difference between people laughing with you and laughing at you.)

Many of the mistakes we make with metaphors can be made with similes as well (and vice versa), so I'm going to use the generic term "figures of speech" again to stand in for both.

Clichéd Figures of Speech

Clichéd figures of speech are just the tip of the iceberg, but they're as common as fleas on a dog. They're a loose cannon in your manuscript. Even if your novel is fit as a fiddle in every other way, go the extra mile and find a fresher way to guild the lily. Just food for thought.

(And, yes, in case you were wondering, I did have way more fun than I should have with that paragraph.)

I mentioned this briefly earlier when I talked about making our figures of speech fresh. The problem with clichéd figures of speech is that we've heard them before. They might have once been fresh and interesting (and probably were or they wouldn't have stuck around long enough to become clichéd), but now we've heard them so many times that they're boring. If there's one thing we don't want our fiction to be, it's boring.

If you're looking for a list of clichéd metaphors and similes, check out the English Club's list of "As...As Similes."

Mixed Figures of Speech

Mixed figures of speech are as groan inducing as a bad comedian without a paddle.

They jumble two or more unrelated metaphors together for a ridiculous and impossible result. They leave the reader confused.

He's burning the midnight oil from both ends.

A leopard can't change his stripes.

When you write a metaphor, make sure all parts contribute to one unified image.

Ambiguous Figures of Speech

An ambiguous figure of speech is one with many potential meanings.

She was like a dog.

If we stop there, the problem is that the reader won't know exactly how to take this. There's too much room for interpretation. This could be a compliment.

She was like a dog, always loyal no matter how many times he lost his temper.

It could be less flattering.

She was like a dog, always in need of a breath mint.

It could be downright insulting.

She was like a dog, not caring who she slept with as long as she got laid.

Unless you expand on what you mean, your reader won't know where you're headed with the metaphor or simile and they'll add their own meaning to it...which may not be the one you intended. Whenever possible, choose a metaphor where the meaning can't be confused.

Inappropriate Figures of Speech

Inappropriate metaphors come in two varieties.

The first is the easiest to avoid. You don't want to introduce an anachronism into your historical fiction, science fiction, or fantasy through your metaphors.

Her memories were lost forever like the treasures buried with the Titanic.

If you're writing a fantasy, did the Titanic exist on your world? If you're writing historical fiction, did the Titanic sink long enough before your story takes place that your hero would be aware of it? If you're writing science fiction, would the Titanic still be as iconic to them as it is to us or would another bigger disaster have supplanted it?

The second inappropriate metaphor happens when our search for a unique turn of phrase blinds us to the connotations of the words we're using.

Her skin glowed pink like the flesh of an ocean salmon.

I can't imagine anyone taking it as a compliment to have their skin compared to a fish. The only way a simile like this works is if your character is a socially awkward fisherman and you're using it to characterize how little he understands women.

Obscure Figures of Speech

I love when an author uses a point of view so deep and intimate even the figures of speech fit the way their character sees and interprets the world.

In a contemporary romance I've been tinkering with, my science teacher character blushes upon meeting her future love interest.

> Her face smoldered as if she'd bent too close over one of the Bunsen burners used in her class.

This works because most of us were in science class. We know what a Bunsen burner is. We can imagine the heat.

It wouldn't work if I wrote the following.

> Her face radiated heat like transuranic elements.

Unless you're a scientist geek, you won't know that transuranic elements are one of the components in highly radioactive material. So while this is an interesting simile (and you could maybe pull it off in a science fiction novel), it doesn't work as well because the simile doesn't add anything more to our understanding than we'd get from "her face radiated heat." The reference is too obscure.

Over-Extended Figures of Speech

Extended metaphors can be extremely powerful, but they're usually used as a tongue-in-cheek form of humor. *The New Yorker* ran a humor piece called "Trade" by Simon Rich in May 2011 that's basically an extended metaphor comparing a baseball trade with being broken up with.

However, not every metaphor is meant to be pushed that far.

> Love is a runaway horse, dragging you by the foot across the prairie until suddenly you break lose and lie shattered on the ground. At night, the coyotes come.

How are all the pieces of this metaphor expected to match up with love?

Extend your metaphors wisely.

CHAPTER THIRTEEN

Describing Setting

S ETTING IS OFTEN UNDERVALUED AND difficult to get right. It's undervalued because people see it as "just description" or think of it as "the boring part." It's difficult to master because we have to find the balance between too much and not enough. We want to bring the story world to life so our readers can imagine it fully, but we don't want it to bog the story down.

A QUICK REMINDER

Setting description works best when we couple it with one of the other "reasons to exist" that we went through in Chapter Three. Descriptions of our setting should also symbolize or foreshadow something, enhance the theme, add subtext, show something about the viewpoint character's personality (through judgments made) or their emotions, add conflict or complications to the story, or hint at the character's backstory. Because we've already gone over all those purposes for description, this chapter isn't going to be me rehashing them with a specific focus on setting. That wouldn't benefit you, and it would waste your time.

I'm also not going to spend this chapter reminding you to use the five senses when describing your settings. Here's your only reminder for that. (Just also remember you don't need to use them all every time. In fact, you shouldn't.)

Instead, this chapter will focus on other techniques we can use to make our setting feel real (even when it's not), seem three-dimensional, and be interesting.

FILL YOUR SETTING WITH EXTRAS AND BACKGROUND NOISE

I'm mentioned this briefly in the chapter on sound, but the principle there applies to setting overall. Imagine watching a movie where the main character went to an amusement park on a sunny summer day and no one else was there. Not only were there no people, but there was no carousel music playing in the background, no screams from people riding the rollercoasters, no laughter from children, no seagulls squawking as they fought over a pile of dropped French fries.

Would that seem realistic or would you think the director had made a major mistake in forgetting to add the extras and the background noise? In any TV show or movie we watch, the production team spends a lot of time making sure spaces feel properly populated and that the normal sounds of the world are playing in the background, whether that's water in the pipes, a car horn, or the annoying guy sitting next to you picking his nails.

When we're writing our setting, we should occasionally add a dash of this as well, without going overboard of course.

How? Glad you asked. I'll give a couple of examples of places and ways we could do this.

Let's say we want to depict the weather. Rather than a "rain poured down" type description, we could have something like this…

The soft *whap, whap, whap* of the windshield wipers filled the car, and in the break the wipers created in the sheets of water pouring over his windows he caught a glimpse of a woman fighting to hold on to her lemon yellow umbrella. The bright splotch of color seemed completely out of place in the rest of the grey city scape. And completely out of place with his mood.

As another example, what do we do with a pause in the conversation? Most likely we default to…

He paused.

But instead of stating that the character paused, we could show that pause by filling it.

"I'm getting a second opinion." The clock on the wall ticked abnormally loud, counting down my limited seconds. "Six months just isn't fair."

There are other ways we can weave in these details, but hopefully those examples have helped you start thinking about the possibilities. Our books shouldn't be set in a ghost town…unless, of course, they're set in a literal ghost town.

SHARE WHAT MAKES YOUR SETTING UNIQUE

No two locations are alike in this world. Some people chose to live in a location because they were born there or because they don't see a way they can leave due to finances or other responsibilities. But many people select the place they want to live based on that spot's specific characteristics.

So what sets our setting apart from the thousands of other places that on the surface might seem just like it? Those details should make it onto the page.

If your story is set in San Francisco, show the street cars. Show the steeply sloping streets. But also show the cultural elements that are distinct—the coffee culture, the giant Mission District burritos, the fog and the wind, the more casual clothes.

If you're writing a science fiction or fantasy story, your job becomes more challenging because you have to create this from scratch. A good trick is to take a real-world culture or location and build off of it.

INCLUDE WHAT THE READER MIGHT GET WRONG

An important element of description is assumption management. We're controlling how our reader experiences our story world so that there are no unintentional misunderstanding. If we fail to properly control the reader's perceptions, it can result in the reader being jerked out of the story or the reader becoming angry or frustrated with our story because their reasonable expectations weren't met. Fiction that we intend to sell isn't about us. It's about the reader and giving them the best possible experience.

So we should ask ourselves what our reader might get wrong. For example, if we say castle, and we mean a castle made out of glass, then we need to include that. Otherwise, our reader will probably imagine a medieval fortress made of stone. If we do mean the traditional medieval stone castle, then we don't need to spend time describing it in depth. In that situation, we can expect that our reader will naturally fill in the correct details.

For our "standard" castle, we'd instead want to look for what sets it apart and makes it interesting. We'd want to filter it through the eyes of our viewpoint character because no two people experience something in exactly the same way. (See Chapter Two.)

Which leads into the next point. Our starting premise for this book was that, unless we're writing in omniscient point of view, everything should be filtered through the unique perspective and personality of our viewpoint character. Each character will experience the world differently from the others. One of the most important things is our character's perception of what's around them rather than the bare facts of what's around them.

We need to be specific enough in describing our setting that our reader experiences what we want them to experience. We can't assume that our reader will understand what we mean if we write something like *a North Dakota winter*, *a Texas sunset*, or *the ocean breeze*.

We can't guarantee that every reader has been there. We're living in a global time. We'll likely have readers from all over the world. Maybe our reader grew up in Florida and hasn't ever seen snow in person. Maybe they've never been to the ocean and they don't know what an ocean breeze feels like or smells like or tastes like on their lips.

Even if they've been there, they experienced it through their perspective, not through our viewpoint character's eyes. That can dramatically change what's noticed and how things are perceived. A lot of the magic behind fiction is controlling the reader experience without letting them see the wizard behind the curtain.

MAKE YOUR SETTING A REFLECTION OF THE PERSON WHO LIVES THERE

What we're talking about here is another layer of symbolism. An excellent example of this is the three major locations in J.R.R. Tolkien's *Lord of the Rings* trilogy—Rivendell, the Shire, and Mordor.

Mordor is the land of the nearly immortal villain Sauron, who wants the world to fall into shadows. It's surrounded by dark mountains, with entry possible only through the Black Gate. Inside Mordor, Sauron's home is much like a volcano.

Whereas the Shire, where the hobbits live, is peaceful and agrarian. The hobbit holes are bright and cozy. It's a place where you can feel safe. It's also the perfect home for the loyal, steady hobbits.

And Rivendell, where the elves live, is hidden from the world, withdrawn just like the elves have withdrawn from the cares of the rest of the world.

THE #1 SECRET: MAKE YOUR READER WANT TO GO THERE

This is the most frequently missed element of setting and yet it's the most important to creating a setting that will live in the reader's mind—make them want to visit your setting.

Whether or not the reader can actually go there is beside the point. What we're trying to tap in to is desire. Because if our reader wants to go there, they'll want to return to our book so that they can feel like they're part of the world.

Even if you're writing about a horrible place, there should be something wonderful about it that the reader wishes they could see and experience.

Middle Earth had the Shire and Rivendell alongside Mordor and the orcs.

Hogwarts had a basilisk that petrified people, moving staircases, a whomping willow that would try to kill you, and a forbidden forest with all manner of frightening creatures in it like the giant spider Aragog, but it also had Quidditch and magic and feasts where you didn't have to cook or wash the dishes after. It had Honeyduke's sweet shop.

Make sure you've found something about your world for readers to fall in love with as well as to fear.

BONUS TIP

If you want extra help bringing your setting to life, I recommend checking out *The Urban Setting Thesaurus: A Writer's Guide to City Spaces* and *The Rural Setting Thesaurus: A Writer's Guide to Personal and Natural Spaces* by Angela Ackerman and Rebecca Puglisi.

CHAPTER FOURTEEN

Describing Characters

WHEN WE TALK ABOUT DESCRIBING characters, we're really looking at two separate issues— describing non-viewpoint characters and describing viewpoint characters. Viewpoint characters (also known as point-of-view characters) are the ones who are telling the story. We see the world through their eyes and this presents us with a particular set of challenges.

Because describing non-viewpoint characters is theoretically easier, I'm going to start with them and move on to how to handle the challenge of describing a viewpoint character in a natural and believable way.

DESCRIBING A NON-VIEWPOINT CHARACTER

I said that describing a non-viewpoint character is *theoretically* easier because at least we're not having them try to believably describe themselves.

The quicksand that many writers fall into when describing a non-viewpoint character is the dossier-style description where the reader receives a list of facts.

> He was almost six feet tall, with red hair and blue eyes, and he walked with a limp. He wore a corduroy jacket and jeans.

People can see this character, and some of the details about him might even be interesting, but the description itself is flat and is something the reader will likely skip or forget.

What we need to do is to find a way to convey the essence of a character's appearance without bogging the story down.

(Many of the examples I'll show you in this chapter employ more than one of these strategies to create high-impact character descriptions, so you'll be able to see the techniques in action more than once.)

Highlight the Interesting or Memorable Features

If you remember back Chapter Five, we talked about how less is often more when it comes to descriptions in general. It's still true when we're trying to describe a character. We don't need an abundance of details. We need the right details. Everything else can be left up to the reader's imagination to fill in.

What stands out about this character? What details will be memorable? What impression do you want them to leave?

Take a look at this example from Susan Kaye Quinn's third *Debt Collector: Season 1* book, *Ecstasy*.

> A man stands in the doorway; at least I think it's a man. His goggles are like mini-telescopes, one protruding from each eye. There's no part of him exposed, from his gloved hands to his masked face to the fine-weave mesh suit that's lumpy

over his clothes. The suit is so bright-white that it glows, making him look like an oversized, electrified bunny.

Everything about this description says *mad scientist*. If she'd diluted it down by describing his height and weight, or by describing everything about him once he removed his mask, we would have lost the impact of this description. Instead, a little later, when he does remove his mask, this is all the additional description we get:

He has one blue eye, one green. The green one seems to glint with its own light.

Not only is this strange and therefore memorable, but the underlying suggestion here is that the green eye might not be real. Susan Kaye Quinn limited her description to give only three details about this man (his goggles, his suit, and his eyes), and all of them are interesting.

They also work together to portray a person who is working to create cybernetic implants. Which leads into our next two points.

Give Your Description a Focal Point

Sometimes what we need to do in order to bring our character description to life and make it stick in the reader's mind is to give the details a unifying focus.

Here's an example from Annie Bellet's urban fantasy *Justice Calling*.

He looked roughly thirty years old and somewhat like a Hollywood version of a Norse God. About six foot six with shaggy white-blond hair, features that a romance novel would call chiseled, and more lean muscle than a CrossFit junkie.

What makes this description work is the first line where she describes him as "a Hollywood version of a Norse God." Marvel's depiction of Thor immediately jumped to my mind when I read that. That single line brings all the other details together to build a focused whole out of what might have otherwise been forgettable.

Hint at the Character's Nature or Make Them Intriguing through the Suggestion that They're Not What They Appear to Be

What details can hint at their nature, their personality, or that their appearance might not reflect the truth about them?

Here's an example from Lindsay Buroker's steampunk novel *Deathmaker*. The viewpoint character is a POW fighter pilot, and she's about to be locked up with the infamous pirate-scientist known as Deathmaker. Her nation hates him because his reputation claims he created the biological agent that basically melted an entire village of their people.

This description is on the long side, but after I'll break down for you why it works.

> The man standing in the doorway, his hands shackled before him, appeared more warrior than scientist, with a hide vest leaving his muscular arms and part of his chest exposed. She had expected a crazy old man with spectacles or magnifying goggles and white hair sticking out in all directions.

> The figure in the doorway appeared to be about thirty, and his long black locks fell down his back in matted ropes. In contrast to the tangled hair, his mustache and goatee were trimmed, and his bronze Cofah skin was clean of grime, but nothing about the dark scowling eyes, the shark-tooth necklace, or the spiked leather cuffs invited one to venture closer.

Like we looked at above, she focuses on the things about his appearance that will make you remember this character, specifically the dreadlocks and the shark-tooth necklace and spiked leather cuffs.

She also contrasts our viewpoint character's expectations with what turns out to be true.

And she does what we're looking at in this point. There's a strong hint that this man is not what he appears to be created by the discontinuity between his tangled hair and the neat and clean remainder of his appearance.

The Description Should Be Colored by Their Relationship with the Protagonist

If our character is meeting their arch nemesis for the first time, the tone of their description should be different than if they were meeting their old flame for the first time in ten years—even if the two men look identical.

Part of this will be word choice, but another part of it will be what details our viewpoint character chooses to notice. When we feel positively toward someone, we're more likely to notice their good elements, and the reverse is true if we feel negatively toward someone. The more we care about a person, the more likely we also are to try to put a positive spin on their less flattering qualities.

Appeal to the Senses

I won't belabor this point because we've already spent chapters on it, but remember that people are more than just their physical appearance. The smell of them, the sound of them, the way they move and the way they feel can often be more memorable and interesting than the simple external visuals.

DESCRIBING THE VIEWPOINT CHARACTER

If you have more than one viewpoint character, they can easily describe the other character when they first meet. If they already know each other, though, or you have only a single viewpoint character, it becomes more challenging.

(It's also easy to handle if you're writing in an omniscient point of view because the omniscient narrator can simply describe the characters. To learn more about point of view, I'd recommend you take a look at *Point of View in Fiction* and *Deep Point of View*.)

Let's look at the "what not to do" ideas first.

The Mirror Cliché

The first time a writer encounters this problem, the default becomes "well, I'll just have them look in the mirror and describe for the reader what they look like."

In terms of maintaining a consistent point of view, we could probably find a way to justify the mirror cliché, but it's been so overused that it feels fake no matter how we rationalize it. The best idea is to leave it out.

The Point-of-View Error

The other two ways that we writers sometimes try to wiggle around the conundrum of describing our viewpoint character is through introducing a point-of-view error.

The most straightforward is the plain info dump. Somewhere early in the book the writer simply describes what the viewpoint character looks like. This is problematic because it feels forced.

The other point-of-view error is what I like to call the *detail slide*. Here's what this looks like.

I braided my long black hair.

Because we don't normally think about the color of our hair, this violates point of view. **So how can we work in the physical details about our viewpoint character in a more natural way?**

Have Them Compare Themselves to Someone Else

This is something we naturally do. So, for example, if our viewpoint character has pancake-flat hair and she meets a woman with beautiful curls, we can show our viewpoint character's appearance through her jealousy over the other woman's looks.

Comparison isn't the same as contrasting though. We can show our viewpoint character's appearance through a similarity as well. Suzanne Collins uses this technique in *The Hunger Games* where Katniss pays attention to her grey eyes because Gale also has grey eyes.

I'll give you a quick example of how this might work.

It was eerie seeing my own blue eyes staring back at me from a stranger's face. I couldn't doubt that she really was my sister.

Use Self-Deprecating Humor about a Physical Flaw

We can get away with a lot if our character is poking fun at themselves. This often happens when they're in a situation where they're self-conscious (see the previous point about comparing themselves to others).

Here's a quick example. Let's say a woman's mother gave her a sundress for her birthday. Now she's headed out to the family picnic, and her mother specifically requests that she wear the "lovely new dress" she bought her.

I slid on the dress. The black-and-white polka dots accentuated my already wide hips. I looked like a Jersey cow.

Have Someone Else Comment on Their Looks

We can also have another character who knows them comment on their looks. We just need to make sure it's natural. That means it should be something the other character would have reason to comment on. If we don't make it fit the context of the story and the personality of the characters involved, it ends up feeling like author intrusion.

Natural reasons could be things like our viewpoint character makes a drastic change in their appearance or our friend character tries to help our viewpoint out. For example, our viewpoint character might have an important date coming up and her friend might make suggestions for what she could wear or on ways to help tame her frizzy hair.

If you're writing a YA novel, teenagers can sometimes be cruel about the appearance of others, which gives you another natural way to weave in physical details.

EXTRA TIP

Janice Hardy wrote an excellent post about describing our character's age at Fiction University. I highly recommend reading it. If you're not able to click the link in the previous sentence, you can go to the Bonus Resources page for this book on my website or you can search for "An Age-Old Question: How Do You Show a Character's Age?" and Janice's name.

CHAPTER FIFTEEN

Describing Actions and Reactions

WHEN MOST OF US THINK ABOUT description, we don't usually think about action. Because it is description, but it isn't. It is description in that we're showing the reader what our viewpoint character sees or feels. It isn't in that it reads differently than does a standard description of the setting, for example. Action is what characters do, rather than how they are.

In this chapter, I'll briefly show you how the principles governing good description apply to writing interesting action as well. I'll also touch on internal action, a special element of fiction that helps readers connect with our characters and adds emotion.

EXTERNAL ACTION

External action comes in two types—voluntary and involuntary. A voluntary action would be something like walking across the room or drinking a glass of water. An involuntary action would be something like the character's hands shaking or the character taking a step backward upon hearing bad news. There's also a grey area where certain actions could be either voluntary or involuntary—a smile, for example.

We need external action in our fiction, but just like anything else, we can slow our book down by including too much of it or make our book less interesting by writing action that's flat, flabby, or clichéd.

Here's how to avoid both those pitfalls.

Be Specific When Possible

Sometimes our character needs to simply walk across the room, but sometimes it'd be better to have them trudge, stomp, or lurch. Sometimes our character will drink a glass of water, but sometimes they should sip or gulp.

Whenever we're writing actions, we should make sure we're describing it in the way that will best allow the reader to imagine what we intended and in the way that will convey the emotion or tone we need.

This can also help us tighten our writing. Instead of writing "he walked quickly" we could decide on what type of "walking quickly" he was doing. Was he striding? Was he marching? Was he storming?

Like everything in writing, the key here is balance. If we overdo this, it'll stand out to the reader, and that's not what we want.

Skip the Obvious

We don't need to describe the minutiae of every move our characters make. Take a look at these two examples.

Example 1: He reached out and turned on the light.

Example 2: He turned on the light.

Example 2 is better. The reaching is implied in the fact that he turned on the light. We don't need to show him reaching.

We can accidentally do this on a larger scale as well.

> She opened the door, left the house, and locked the door behind her. She climbed into her car.

We don't need the blow by blow here. Unless the fact that she locked the door behind her will be important to the story later, we can simply write...

> She left the house and climbed into her car.

The fact that she opened the door and locked it behind her are obvious and don't need to be included.

We can also often suggest movement without having to describe all of it. Say we have a jewel thief who managed to steal a priceless gem right off the neck of the woman wearing it. He's now home with his prize, and he's in a back room ready to verify its authenticity.

> He set up his binocular microscope. Before he called his buyer, he needed to make sure the thing wasn't a fake. His knuckles ached every time the weather turned thanks to the one time he'd made that mistake.
> The doorbell rang, and he dumped the jewel back into his pocket. He wasn't expecting anyone.
> "Just a minute."
> He tucked his gun into the back of his pants and opened the door. The woman he'd nabbed the jewel from stood on his front step.

Even though we don't tell the reader that he walked across his house, they'll be able to fill it in based on what we do share.

What we don't want to skip in terms of action description are the steps the reader needs to understand what's happening. For example, like this...

> Declan chased Amy out to the front yard.
> "Bet you can't catch me," Amy said from the branches of a tree.

We've skipped the step where Amy got up the tree in the first place, and that's not something obvious that the reader will naturally fill in the same way they can fill in the fact that our character must have crossed a room to open a door or must have reached out before shaking someone's hand.

Only Describe Action that Matters

If our character comes home from work and what matters is finding the dead body planted in their kitchen, we don't first need to see them take off their coat and shoes, set aside their keys, take a trip to the restroom, check their phone messages, and then finally head to the kitchen.

Just send them to the kitchen already! (No one wants to see all the things our character does in the bathroom anyway.)

Each action should serve a strong purpose within the story. Does the reader need to see it happening? Does it matter in some way?

Include Body Language

Do you remember that line from Disney's *The Little Mermaid* about not underestimating the power of body language? (Tell me you didn't hear Ursula's voice just now.)

Body language is an incredibly powerful form of communication in real life, and in fiction it's an incredibly powerful form of action and description because it shows rather than tells. Body language can be interpreted (and misinterpreted) by our viewpoint character as they make assumptions about the people around them.

Body language also helps us pace our writing, and it adds emotional depth to the situations we place our characters in.

The problem many writers have is that they default to the empty, overused forms of body language like smiling, nodding, frowning, sighing, hands running through hair, or arms being crossed.

Body language can do so much more, but it requires that we work at finding bits of body language to share that feel new and yet authentic. A good exercise is to watch people when they're not aware of you. You'll see them tugging on their earlobes, bobbing their crossed leg, picking at their cuticles, and many other small ticks. Also watch the way people's bodies telegraph their emotions. How do they hold themselves when they're excited compared to when they're angry or sad?

I mentioned the two setting thesauri by Angela Ackerman and Rebecca Puglisi in the chapter on setting, but they have *The Emotion Thesaurus* as well. It's a useful tool to help us develop body language that can hint at what our non-viewpoint characters are thinking and feeling.

Another way to approach body language is to amplify an overused bit of body language to make it fresh again. For example…

> Bridget sucked in her lips until they vanished. The smile that returned to her face looked chiseled in stone and painted on, fake as the statues in church.

It's still a smile, but it's so much more because now it's also the viewpoint character's interpretation of her smile.

INTERNAL REACTIONS

Internal reactions are bodily responses we have no control over—dizziness, a racing heart, sweaty palms, tense shoulders, a clenched stomach, etc. (Internal dialogue—the character thinking to themselves—is also internal, but we're talking about action in this chapter, not about dialogue.)

Here's an example from *Ashes* by Ilsa J. Bick. The viewpoint character, Alex, is recovering from a burst of extreme pain.

> ...she hung there on all fours, exhausted, a sparkling sensation of pins and needles coursing through her veins and prickling her skin as if her entire body had fallen asleep and her brain had only now figured out how to reconnect. Her heart was hammering, and the inside of her head felt slushy and bruised.

Internal reactions like this are involuntary or instinctive, and they happen in response to a stimulus of either a thought or an event. While we can sometimes manage them once they happen, they initially come without our conscious decision or will.

These involuntary responses are also the expression of emotions. It's the way our body feels inside when we're gripped by hatred for the drunk driver who killed our friend. It's the rush of excitement or love. It's the paralyzing hit of fear. But instead of naming (i.e. telling) those emotions, these visceral reactions allow us to show them to the reader.

They're a major element in engaging the reader's emotions.

Here's how to best use internal, visceral reactions.

Don't Overuse Them

Think about visceral reactions as cayenne pepper. A dash adds a special bite to your dish. A scoop burns out your taste buds and ensures you won't want to eat that dish again. If you've ever read a book where the character's heart pounded so often you were worried they were about to have a heart attack, you know what I mean. Make sure to save them for important moments.

Add Variety

When we first start adding visceral reactions, it can be easy to default to phrases like "her heart pounded" and to repeat those pet visceral reactions too often. Our bodies react in a variety of ways, and we should make use of the full spectrum.

Beware of Interpreting Them

Sometimes it's alright to both show and tell, but this is the exception, not the norm. So when we're adding visceral reactions, we should usually give the evidence and stop.

Showing and Telling: Her hands shook with fear.

Showing Alone: Her hands shook.

Context will allow the reader to understand them.

Personalize It

One of the internal sensations for agitation is feeling overheated. How will our character describe that sensation? A middle-aged woman with a good sense of humor might think of it in terms of getting a taste of the hot flashes she'll experience in menopause. A teenager might liken it to when the air conditioning broke—For Three. Whole. Days.

Same sensation. Different points of view. Infinite possibilities.

Remember that They're Always Reactions to a Stimulus

Unless we're sick, we don't just start shaking out of the blue. Something triggers that reaction. Maybe it's the thought that we left the gas stove on at home. Or maybe it's that we spotted the ex who cheated on us in the next grocery aisle. They don't happen without a reason, and the reader needs to see that reason.

CHAPTER SIXTEEN

Take It to the Page

I N EACH OF MY *BUSY WRITER'S GUIDES*, I LIKE to include checklists, questions, or other editing helps to make it easier for you to apply what you've learned to your own project. If you'd like a downloadable/printable copy of the Take It to the Page exercises, you can find them at www.marcykennedy.com/description. The password is **wordpainting**.

When it comes to description, part of what we'll be trying to do is identify the areas where you're already strong and the areas that you need to work on. That way you can spend your time fixing the weaker spots.

Depending on how much time you have available, you have two options.

Option 1: If you're short on time, pick three chapters—your opening chapter, a chapter from the middle of your book, and a chapter closer to the end. Don't select your best. Choose randomly. You'll be applying the Take It to the Page exercises to those chapters. Once you've identified the areas where you struggle, you can work on those throughout the rest of your book.

Option 2: If you have the time or if you know that description is a challenge for you, you can run your entire book through this process.

Now that you've decided whether to use a few chapters or your whole book, go through and mark every description, excluding action. You're only going to be marking up your sensory description for now.

To save trees, I like to simply change the font color in my document, but you could also print out the pages you'll be working with and underline the descriptions or mark them in the margins. (I don't recommend highlighting because we'll be using highlighting later to check for the five senses.)

Step 1

Check the beginning of each scene. Have you grounded the reader in the setting within the first couple of paragraphs? This grounding is important to do because the harder a reader needs to work to figure out the *when* and *where*, the less attention they're paying to what's important and the more likely they are to close the book.

If you haven't changed locations between scenes, then you won't always need to do this or you'll only need to do so briefly. If you have changed locations, you always need to reorient the reader to the new location.

Step 2

For every description you use, ask yourself the following questions to decide whether this description should stay or be cut. You want each passage to do at least two of the things listed below.

It's best not to slow yourself down by trying to change your descriptions as you go through this step. Instead, I recommend marking each description with either a check mark or an X. That way you can come back to the X passages later.

- Do I need to include this to ground the reader in the setting (time, place, and culture)?
- Does this passage of description symbolize or foreshadow something important to the story? Does it enhance the theme or add subtext?
- Does this description show something about the character because they've noticed it (or because of what they notice about it)?
- Do the viewpoint character's emotions come through in the way this description is worded?
- Does this description add conflict or complications for my viewpoint character?
- Does this hint at my viewpoint character's backstory?

Step 3

For the descriptions that passed Step 2, ask yourself the following question.

Is this the right time to include this description or am I unnecessarily slowing the pace of the scene?

Step 4

For the descriptions that are still standing, it's time to look at their content.

- Do your descriptions include ten-dollar words? Try to find a simpler alternative.
- Do your descriptions include clichés? Try to find a fresher way to say it.

- Do you include too many figures of speech? Keep the best and cut the rest.
- Do your descriptions include flowery abstractions? Try to find a clearer way to say it.
- Have you included a lot of adverbs or adjectives? Remove the ones that are redundant or replace them with a stronger descriptor.
- Have you over-described (including too many details)? Select the ones that will be most interesting and leave the strongest image with the reader, and delete the rest.
- Are your descriptions general rather than specific? Picture in your mind exactly what you want to show the reader, and add those details.
- Have you told rather than shown? Find a way to show in your description instead.

Step 5

Even if you're running your whole manuscript through these checks, I recommend you do this step for three chapters first. Assign each sense a different color and circle or highlight every time you use a sense.

Once you finish, spread the papers out around you or zoom out in your word processing program so that you can see multiple pages at a time. You'll immediately be able to see which sense you use the most and where you're weak.

Use this information to guide your edits for the rest of the document.

Step 6

Now it's time to examine each of the senses you've used to see if you can make them more powerful. If you've neglected a sense, you can also use this checklist to decide on a way to add it in.

Sight

- Have you allowed your viewpoint character to put their own twist on it?
- Could you put what you're showing into motion?
- Could you break expectations by playing with opposites?
- Is there a way you could make this passage more interesting by describing shapes, textures, patterns, depth, shadows, or optical illusions?
- Does what your character visually notice first match with their gender?
- If you're describing a group, have you focused on *the one* rather than on *the many*?
- Have you properly ordered your description in the way a person would normally notice things?

Sound

- Could you use a word that sounds like its meaning to create an echo?
- Does this sound have an emotional effect on your viewpoint character? Should it?
- Does the sound match the mood you're trying to create?
- Have you included background noise?

Taste

- Did you name a taste when you should have described it? Have you described a taste that needed to only be named?

- Could you bring this to life through a metaphor or other comparison?
- Have you added an element of surprise?
- Are you able to go beyond simple taste and add texture?

Smell

- Have you waited too long to describe the smell? Scents should be described when they're fresh, otherwise we go "nose blind" to them.
- Could this smell alert your viewpoint character to an impeding change or danger?
- Have you connected the smell to an emotion?
- Would your story be stronger if you added a showpiece scent?
- Have you contrasted a good smell with a bad one?

Touch

- Have you used aspects of touch like temperature, texture, pressure, and moisture?
- If your story is lacking in touch, could you explore non-physical touch in some way?
- Should you break the continuum of intimacy?
- How does your character interpret the touch?

Remember that you don't need to do all of these things for every description that you use. The idea is to make sure that for each description you've done something to keep it interesting for the reader.

Step 7

Do a search for the words *saw, smelled, tasted, touched, felt,* and *heard.* (If you're writing in present tense, you'll need to change the tense to match.) Have you used these words as part of a simile or to try to describe one of the five senses?

If they're part of a simile, is the simile you've created fresh and interesting or is it a cliché?

If you've used them to try to describe one of the five senses, can you make it more vivid and immediate by rewriting the sentence without *saw, smelled, tasted, touched, felt,* or *heard*?

Step 8

Examine your descriptions of your settings and ask yourself the following questions:

- Are your settings populated with people and filled with background noise?
- Have you included the elements that make your setting unique?
- Have you shown any details the reader might get wrong?
- Does the setting reflect the person who lives there?
- What about your setting will make your reader want to go there?

Step 9

Look at your descriptions of your non-viewpoint characters.

- Have you highlighted the interesting or memorable features?
- Does your description have a focal point?
- Have you used contrast to add intrigue or tension?
- Have you appealed to the senses?
- Is the description colored by how your viewpoint character feels about the character they're describing?

Step 10

Look at your descriptions of your viewpoint characters. Have you used the mirror cliché? Have you introduced a point-of-view error in your description?

If so, try to correct it using one of the following techniques:

- Have them compare themselves to someone else.
- Use self-deprecating humor about a physical flaw.
- Have another character comment (naturally of course) on their appearance.

Step 11

In Step 12, you're going to be focusing on a few chapters, but first you need to get an idea of whether or not you tend to overuse generic body language.

Run a search for the following words (and their variants). If you're using Microsoft Word for this, the Find panel is excellent because it not only tells you how many times you've used these words, but it shows them to you in a list.

- nod
- smile
- frown
- shook (usually followed by "his/her head")

If you find you've overused a generic piece of body language, find a more interesting replacement or expand on your generic body language to make it fresh again.

Step 12

Even if you're working through your whole manuscript, I recommend you start with two to three chapters for this step. You're going to be reading through them, paying attention to your internal reactions and external action. For this step, we're going to focus on external actions. When you come to an internal reaction, highlight it, but then move on. We'll come back to them in a minute.

As you read through, have you described obvious actions that the reader doesn't need to see? Make sure that you're only showing important actions.

Do you see any other types of body language that you tend to overuse? Run a search and see how many times you've used these pieces of body language.

Step 13

Look at the internal reactions you highlighted on your way through your sample chapters.

- How often have you used them? Does it look like you're overusing them?
- Is there variety or do you have a lot of pounding hearts (for example)?
- Have you personalized it to reflect the personality and background of your viewpoint character?
- Have you left it at showing, or have you told the emotion as well? We normally want to avoid telling.
- Do they come as a reaction to a stimulus?

APPENDIX A

Showing and Telling

T HE FOLLOWING EXCERPTS COME FROM MY
book *Showing and Telling in Fiction.* Because I know that not
everyone who reads this book will have also read that one, I
decided it would help to include a bit about the topic here. Showing
is a foundational principle of writing good description.

WHAT DO WE MEAN BY SHOWING?

Showing happens when we let the reader experience things for
themselves, through the perspective of the characters. Jeff Gerke,
former owner of Marcher Lord Press, explains showing in one simple question: **Can the camera see it?**[2]

While I love that way of looking at it, we'd really have to ask **can
the camera see it, hear it, smell it, touch it, taste it, or think it?**
(And that would be a strange camera.) Because of that, I prefer to
think about showing as being in a *Star Trek* holodeck.

---

[2] Jeff Gerke, *The First 50 Pages* (Cincinnati: Writer's Digest Books, 2011),
40.

For those of you who aren't as nerdy as I am, a holodeck is a virtual reality room where users can act as a character in a story, which is fully projected using photons and force fields. You can play Jane Eyre or *Twilight*'s Bella or Lee Child's Jack Reacher.

What the user experiences is what they can see, hear, touch, taste, or smell. In holodecks, you can smell things and you can eat or drink "replicated" food. It's a completely immersive experience. To the holodeck user, the experience seems real in all respects. And if you turn the holodeck safety systems off, you can be injured or even die.

When you're faced with deciding whether something is showing or telling, ask yourself this question: **If this were a holodeck program, would I be able to experience this?**

Let's take a couple examples and test them out. A straightforward one first.

> Kate realized she'd locked her keys in the car.

Now, you're standing in the holodeck. What do you experience?

...Nothing. We can't see "realized." We don't know how she knows her keys are locked in the car. Anything we might visualize is something we've had to add because the author didn't. There's no picture here.

Here's one possible showing version...

> Kate yanked on the car door handle. The door didn't budge, and her keys dangled from the ignition. "Dang it!"

You don't have to tell us Kate realized her keys were locked inside her car because we're right there with her. We see her figure it out.

Let's take a more challenging example. This time you're in the holodeck, playing the character of Linda. (Remember that, since you're Linda, you can hear her thoughts, as well as see, smell, hear, taste, and feel what she does.)

First the "telling" version.

> Linda stood at the edge of the Grand Canyon. Though her head spun from the height, she was amazed by the grandeur of it and felt a sense of excitement. Finally she'd taken a big step toward overcoming her fear of heights.

What do you physically experience in the holodeck? Only the Grand Canyon. If you don't know what the Grand Canyon looks like, you can't see even that. None of the rest can appear around you. None of it is her thoughts. They're all abstractions. What does being amazed by the grandeur look like? What does excitement feel like? What does her fear of heights feel like?

If we're in the holodeck, it's going to play out something more like this...

> Linda gripped the damp metal railing that ringed the horseshoe-shaped walkway over the Grand Canyon. Her vision blurred, and she drew in a deep breath and puffed it out the way the instructor taught her in Lamaze class. If it worked for childbirth, it should work to keep her from passing out now. She forced her gaze down to the glass floor. Thick bands of rust red and tan alternated their way down canyon walls that looked as if they'd been chiseled by a giant sculptor. The shaking in her legs faded. She had to get a picture to take back to her kids.

You can see what's around Linda, and you sense her amazement at the size of the canyon, as well as feel her fear. Emotionally you move with her from fear to wonder to excitement as she thinks about sharing it with her children. We hear it in her thoughts. This is the trick to good internal dialogue. It's what your character is thinking at that moment, the way they would think it. It's like you've planted a listening device in their brain and can play their thoughts on a speaker.

So the next time you're not sure whether you're showing or telling, ask "What would I experience in a holodeck?" That's how you should write it if you want to show rather than tell.

WHAT IS TELLING?

The simple answer would be to say that telling is everything that's not showing, but that's not exact enough for me. What I like to do is compare telling and showing when defining telling.

If showing presents evidence to the reader and allows them to draw their own conclusions, telling dictates a conclusion to the reader, telling them what to believe. It states a fact.

Bob was angry…dictates a conclusion.

But what was the evidence?

Bob punched his fist into the wall.

The Black Plague ravaged the country…dictates a conclusion.

But what was the evidence?

You could describe men loading dead bodies covered in oozing black sores onto a wagon. Your protagonist could press a handkerchief filled with posies to her nose and mouth as she passes someone who's drawing in ragged, labored breaths.

Either of those details, or many others, would show the Black Death ravaging the country.

WHY IS SHOWING NORMALLY BETTER THAN TELLING?

Now that we're clear on the difference between showing and telling, I want to go through why showing is normally better. I think understanding this will help us know when to show and when to tell.

Please notice I said <u>normally</u> better. Later, I'm going to talk about times when telling is actually better than showing.

So normally, showing is better than telling because of the experience it gives to the reader.

Showing respects the reader's intelligence. Telling assumes that they're not smart enough to understand unless you lay your story out like a lesson plan. We want something explained to us step by step when we're learning a new concept. For example, if you're learning how to solve calculus equations, you want your teacher to tell you how to work through each type of equation. You don't want them to just show you some examples and leave you to work out the bigger principles for yourself. But fiction isn't supposed to be like a lesson in school. Our primary goal isn't to teach—that's what non-fiction books are for.

Showing entertains the reader. The primary goal of fiction is to entertain. This isn't to say that fiction can't also contain deeper messages. The best fiction does. But it shares those themes through a story. Rather than telling us self-sacrifice is good, it shows us a story of self-sacrifice and allows us to draw our conclusions from that. Think of it this way. If you're a sports fan, what's more entertaining—watching the game yourself or having someone tell you about the game? If you have a favorite TV show, which is more entertaining—watching the show yourself or having someone tell you what happened?

Showing evokes emotion in the reader. If I told you I was sad, what would you feel? Maybe a little pity for me (if you're a softy). But you're not emotionally invested if I only tell you what I'm feeling. If you see my sadness, watch me struggle with it, and learn the details, suddenly it might touch your heart enough that you find yourself crying along with me. That's what you want your readers to do. That's what showing does. It gives them a vicarious experience.

Showing makes your writing interactive. From telling stories around the campfire where the storyteller makes the listeners jump to voting for our favorites to win the latest reality TV competition to video games where we create an avatar that looks like us and reacts to our movements, human beings want to interact with what's around them. Showing allows them to do this by actively engaging their minds as they interpret what's happening. And a reader who feels like they're participating in the story is a reader who won't be able to put it down.

In a talk he did for TED, Andrew Stanton, who worked as a writer on movies like *Finding Nemo*, *Toy Story*, and *WALL-E*, pointed out that "the audience actually wants to work for their meal. They just don't want to know that they're doing that. That's your job as a storyteller—to hide the fact that you're making them work for their meal. We're born problem-solvers. We're compelled to deduct and to deduce because that's what we do in real life."

If you'd like to listen to his whole talk, you can find it at the link below.

http://www.ted.com/playlists/62/how_to_tell_a_story.html

This concept of making the audience work a little but keeping it subtle enough that they don't realize that's what's happening is why we need to know when to show (in other words, when to make them work for their meal) and when to tell (keeping it easy enough for them to follow along so that they don't realize they're doing it).

Other Books by Marcy Kennedy

FOR WRITERS

Deep Point of View

Do you want readers to be so caught up in your book that they forget they're reading?

Then you need deep POV.

Deep POV takes the reader and places them inside of our characters—hearing their thoughts, feeling their emotions, and living the story through them. Compared to other writing styles, it builds a stronger emotional connection between the reader and our characters, creates the feeling of a faster pace, and helps avoid point-of-view errors and telling rather than showing.

In *Deep Point of View*, writing instructor and fiction editor Marcy Kennedy brings her years of experience into showing you how to write deep POV. You'll learn specific, practical things you can do immediately to take your fiction to the next level.

Each book in the *Busy Writer's Guide* series is intended to give you enough theory so that you can understand why things work and why they don't, but also enough examples to see how that theory looks in practice. In addition, they provide tips and exercises to help you take it to the pages of your own story, with an editor's-eye view. Most importantly, they cut the fluff so that you have more time to write and to live your life.

Internal Dialogue

Internal dialogue is the voice inside our heads that we can't ignore, even when we want to. We second-guess ourselves, pass judgment on the world around us, and are at our most emotionally vulnerable. And the same needs to be true for our characters.

Internal dialogue is one of the most powerful tools in a fiction writer's arsenal. It's an advantage we have over TV and movie script writers and playwrights. It's also one of the least understood and most often mismanaged elements of the writing craft.

In *Internal Dialogue: A Busy Writer's Guide*, you'll learn...

- the difference between internal dialogue and narration,
- best practices for formatting internal dialogue,
- ways to use internal dialogue to advance your story,
- how to balance internal dialogue with external action,
- clues to help you decide whether you're overusing or underusing internal dialogue,
- tips for dealing with questions in your internal dialogue,
- and much more!

Showing and Telling in Fiction

You've heard the advice "show, don't tell" until you can't stand to hear it anymore. Yet fiction writers of all levels still seem to struggle with it.

There are three reasons for this. The first is that this isn't an absolute rule. Telling isn't always wrong. The second is that we lack a clear way of understanding the difference between showing and telling. The third is that we're told "show, don't tell," but we're often left without practical ways to know how and when to do that, and how and when not to. So that's what this book is about.

Chapter One defines showing and telling and explains why showing is normally better.

Chapter Two gives you eight practical ways to find telling that needs to be changed to showing and guides you in understanding how to make those changes.

Chapter Three explains how telling can function as a useful first-draft tool.

Chapter Four goes in-depth on the seven situations when telling might be a better choice than showing.

Chapter Five provides you with practical editing tips to help you take what you've learned to the pages of your current novel or short story.

Showing and Telling in Fiction: A Busy Writer's Guide also includes three appendices covering how to use *The Emotion Thesaurus*, dissecting an example so you can see the concepts of showing vs. telling in action, and explaining the closely related topic of As-You-Know-Bob Syndrome.

Dialogue

To write great fiction, you need to know how to write dialogue that shines.

You know the benefits strong dialogue can bring to a story—a faster pace, greater believability, increased tension, and even humor.

But you might not know how to achieve it.

In *Dialogue: A Busy Writer's Guide*, writing instructor and fiction editor Marcy Kennedy brings her years of experience into showing you how to write dialogue that grabs readers and keeps them turning pages.

Inside you'll discover…

- how to format your dialogue to keep it clear and easy to follow,
- tricks to avoid the dreaded As-You-Know-Bob Syndrome,
- how to use dialogue to manage your pace, increase tension, and bring your characters to life,
- the secrets to dealing with dialogue challenges such as dialect, starting a chapter with dialogue, and using contractions in historical fiction and fantasy, and
- much more.

Grammar for Fiction Writers

Not your same old boring grammar guide! This book is fun, fast, and focused on writing amazing fiction.

The world of grammar is huge, but fiction writers don't need to know all the nuances to write well. In fact, some of the rules you were taught in English class will actually hurt your fiction writing, not help it.

Grammar for Fiction Writers won't teach you things you don't need to know. It's all about the grammar that's relevant to you as you write your novels and short stories.

Here's what you'll find inside:

- **Punctuation Basics** including the special uses of dashes and ellipses in fiction, common comma problems, how to format your dialogue, and untangling possessives and contractions.
- **Knowing What Your Words Mean and What They Don't** including commonly confused words, imaginary words and phrases, how to catch and strengthen weak words, and using connotation and denotation to add powerful subtext to your writing.
- **Grammar Rules Every Writer Needs to Know and Follow** such as maintaining an active voice and making the best use of all the tenses for fast-paced writing that feels immediate and draws the reader in.
- **Special Challenges for Fiction Writers** like reversing cause and effect, characters who are unintentionally doing the impossible, and orphaned dialogue and pronouns.
- **Grammar "Rules" You Can Safely Ignore When Writing Fiction**

Point of View in Fiction

It's the opinions and judgments that color everything the reader believes about the world and the story. It's the voice of the character that becomes as familiar to the reader as their own. It's what makes the story real, believable, and honest.

Yet, despite its importance, point-of-view errors are the most common problem for fiction writers.

In *Point of View in Fiction: A Busy Writer's Guide*, you'll learn...

- the strengths and weaknesses of the four different points of view you can choose for your story (first person, second person, limited third person, and omniscient),

- how to select the right point of view for your story,
- how to maintain a consistent point of view throughout your story,
- practical techniques for identifying and fixing head-hopping and other point-of-view errors,
- the criteria to consider when choosing the viewpoint character for each individual scene or chapter,
- and much more!

FICTION

Frozen: Two Suspenseful Short Stories

Twisted sleepwalking.

A frozen goldfish in a plastic bag.

And a woman afraid she's losing her grip on reality.

"A Purple Elephant" is a suspense short story about grief and betrayal.

In "The Replacements," a prodigal returns home to find that her parents have started a new family, one with no room for her. This disturbing suspense short story is about the lengths to which we'll go to feel like we're wanted, and how we don't always see things the way they really are.

ABOUT THE AUTHOR

Marcy Kennedy is a science fiction, fantasy, and suspense author, freelance editor, and writing instructor who believes there's always hope. Sometimes you just have to dig a little harder to find it. In a world that can be dark and brutal and unfair, hope is one of our most powerful weapons.

She writes novels that encourage people to keep fighting. She wants to let them know that no one is beyond redemption and that, in the end, good always wins.

She writes books for writers to give them the courage to keep trying. She wants to let them know that they can achieve their dream of creating fantastic stories.

She's also a proud Canadian and the proud wife of a former U.S. Marine; owns four cats, two birds, and a dog who weighs as much as she does; and plays board games and the flute (not at the same time). Sadly, she's also addicted to coffee and jelly beans.

You can find her blogging at www.marcykennedy.com about writing and about the place where real life meets science fiction, fantasy, and myth. To sign up for her new-release mailing list, please go to the link below. Not only will you hear about new releases before anyone else, but you'll also receive exclusive discounts and freebies. Your email address will never be shared, and you can unsubscribe at any time.

Newsletter: http://eepurl.com/Bk2Or
Website: www.marcykennedy.com
Email: marcykennedy@gmail.com
Facebook: www.facebook.com/MarcyKennedyAuthor

Printed in Great Britain
by Amazon